The Northern Rugby Football Union

THE BIRTH OF RUGBY LEAGUE

The Northern Rugby Football Union
THE BIRTH OF RUGBY LEAGUE
1895 to 1922

LES HOOLE

First published 2019 by DB Publishing, an imprint of JMD Media Ltd,
Nottingham, United Kingdom.

ISBN 978-1-78091-585-2

Printed in the UK

CONTENTS

ACKNOWLEDGEMENTS

The seeds of this book were sown years ago when my passion for Rugby League led to a fascination with the game's early history. My father, grandfather and uncles were all avid followers of Wakefield Trinity, our local team. They would all tell me stories of the skilful players and games they had seen and of players they worked underground with at Lofthouse Colliery. My Dad often told me stories of working underground alongside the Trinity forward Len Bratley on Friday then watching him play at Belle Vue on Saturday afternoon. Eventually I discovered the works of a group of Rugby league historians: Trevor Delaney, Robert Gate, Alex Service, Andrew Hardcastle, Michael Latham, Tom Mather, Graham Morris. Stephen Wild and Tony Collins, who were writing about the birth of Rugby League and gave me the inspiration.

I would like to thank Michael Latham for his help, encouragement and his superb work checking the manuscript for errors, Professor Tony Collins for writing the excellent foreword, and I would like to thank the following for allowing me to use images from their collections: Dave Makin, Tim Auty, Michael Latham, Paul Hicks, Bernard Shooman. Stuart Quinn. Rob Grillo. Peter Benson and Stephen Wild. And not forgetting my wife Dianne, who has tolerated nothing but the Northern Union for the last year and is now an expert in the deeds of Billy Batten, James Lomas and Harold Wagstaff. And the members of the Facebook group Rugby League Historians who have shared images and information and particularly those bold northern newspaper editors and reporters who stood in face of the opposition and prejudice from the Rugby Union establishment and had great conviction in the new code and honestly chronicled the formation and deeds of the Northern Rugby Football Union.

FOREWORD

When the Northern Union (NU) was founded in August 1895 it was stepping into the unknown. No sport had ever split in two like rugby had, and no-one could know what the future would hold. The new organisation was conceived in rebellion and born in bravery. In this wonderful new book, Les Hoole has brought to life the spirit of those pioneering days when Rugby League was the Northern Union.

The Northern Union may have been new, but it had deep roots. Clubs like Bradford, Hull, Rochdale and Swinton had been formed in the 1860s, a full generation before the birth of the NU. The Yorkshire Cup, which began in 1877 with an historic triumph by Halifax, established many of the traditions we take for granted: knock-out cups, local rivalries, fanatical supporters and a shared sense of community. By the time the first NU season kicked off, rugby was well-established as the sport of choice and the expression of local pride in dozens of cities, towns and villages across the north of England.

It was a social phenomenon as much as it was a sporting story. The NU had the best rugby players, the best clubs, and, as the game evolved, the best rules. It was proof that working-class people across the industrial north of England were not the second-class citizens that their social superiors portrayed them to be. If you wanted to play in the NU, you had to be outstanding. So, it was no surprise that one of the highest compliments that could be paid to somebody or something was to say that it 'were best int Northern Union'.

There could be no doubt about the brilliance of the NU's players and clubs. As can be seen throughout this book, the game already had superstars like Jim Lomas, Albert Goldthorpe, Jack Fish and Harold Wagstaff, and powerhouse clubs like Broughton Rangers, Oldham and Huddersfield. The impact of these trailblazers can be gauged by the fact that the names of Goldthorpe and Wagstaff live on in rugby league even today in the 21st century.

A little more than a decade after rugby had split in Britain, the Northern Union game was born in New Zealand and Australia. Just as the rules of the NU had spread down under, so too did its principles. This was a game that was open to all, regardless of your school, job or social status. As Harry Hoyle, one of the founders of Australian rugby league, put it, 'the set of conditions controlling the [rugby] union are not suitable to the democracy and social conditions of the Australian people'. The same was true wherever rugby league was played.

It is almost 100 years since the Northern Union changed its name to the Rugby Football League in 1922. Les Hoole, in this book, has illuminated the rich and vibrant life of the world that the pioneers of the Northern Union created. We should all be grateful for their vision, foresight and courage.

Let those who drink the water salute those who dug the well.

Tony Collins, April 2019

Chapter 1

EARLY DAYS – 1895 TO 1900

Harry Waller, a textile mill owner and prominent member of the Liberal Party in West Yorkshire, was a passionate believer in the Northern Union. In his opening address as newly elected chairman of the meeting at the George Hotel, Huddersfield, on 29 August 1895 his passion and enthusiasm for the breakaway came to the fore when made the following statement:

'Rugby football in the North cannot be honestly carried out under the existing by-laws of the English Rugby Union. A new Rugby Union, the Northern Union, must be formed.'

Harry Waller, a shrewd and gifted organiser, then sought the opinions of the delegates gathered in the room and made the following proposal:

'That the clubs here represented decide to form a Northern Rugby Football Union, and pledge themselves to push forward, without delay, its establishment on the principle of payment for bona-fide broken-time only.'

The proposal was carried and Waller then made the statement:

'I declare the motion carried. We will now resign from the Rugby Football Union and proceed to build the Northern Union.'

Dewsbury decided not to join, however, and the Union's membership was made up to 22 when Stockport, who had communicated with a telegram to the meeting, were admitted and Runcorn joined at a subsequent meeting of the committee.

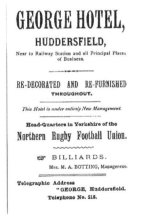

The George Hotel, Huddersfield was the venue for the meeting of 21 of the leading Yorkshire- and Lancashire-based Rugby Union clubs which led to the formation of the Northern Rugby football Union. The hotel, which is a grade II listed building, was designed by William Walker and was built around 1851.

NORTHERN RUGBY FOOTBALL LEAGUE

		P	W	D	L	Pts	F	A
1	Manningham	42	33	0	9	66	367	158
2	Halifax	42	30	5	7	65	312	139
3	Runcorn	42	24	8	10	56	314	143
4	Oldham	42	27	2	13	56	374	194
5	Brighouse R.	42	22	9	11	53	247	129
6	Tyldesley	42	21	8	13	50	260	164
7	Hunslet	42	24	2	16	50	279	207
8	Hull	42	23	3	16	49	259	158
9	Leigh	42	21	4	17	46	214	269
10	Wigan	42	19	7	16	45	245	147
11	Bradford	42	18	9	15	45	254	175
12	Leeds	42	20	3	19	43	258	247
13	Warrington	42	17	5	20	39	198	240
14	St. Helens*	42	15	8	19	36	195	230
15	Liversedge	42	15	4	23	34	261	355
16	Widnes	42	14	4	24	32	177	323
17	Stockport	42	12	8	22	32	171	315
18	Batley	42	12	7	23	31	137	298
19	Wakefield T.	42	13	4	25	30	156	318
20	Huddersfield	42	10	4	28	24	194	274
21	Broughton R.	42	8	8	26	24	165	244
22	Rochdale H.	42	4	8	30	16	78	388

* St. Helens were deducted 2 points.

The scoring system was try, 3 points; conversion, 2 points; penalty goal, 3 points; drop-goal, 4 points.

Following the momentous decision made in Huddersfield, the Northern Union quickly formed an emergency committee to create a fixture list for the 22 clubs involved in the first season. The committee met on 3 September at the Spread Eagle Hotel in Manchester and remarkably the very first games took place on 7 September.

The final league table for the first season.

Manningham were the very first Northern Union Champions; the long and exhausting season was decided on the final weekend of fixtures when

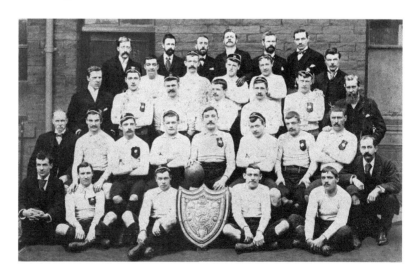

Manningham's victory at Hunslet gave the Bradford-based team a single-point advantage over their nearest rivals Halifax. Manningham were also champions of the Yorkshire Senior Competition, the trophy with which they are pictured, which ran alongside the main Northern Rugby Football League.

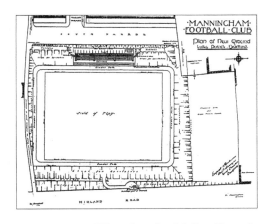

The plan for Valley Parade, the Manningham football club's ground.

Fred Clegg, described in contemporary press reports as a 'dashing forward', was one of the fine pack of forwards that Manningham had assembled during the club's Rugby Union era. Clegg made 40 appearances during the first season of Northern Union football, scoring seven tries. His form during the season led to him being selected for two appearances for the Yorkshire representative team.

George Edward Lorimer was a proud Bradfordian, born in Manningham on 26 February 1872, just a hundred yards from Valley Parade. A tall, slimly built youth, he began his rugby career with Manningham Free Wanderers as a centre and a few seasons later he moved to Heaton and then on to Manningham Clarence. He was then invited to join the Manningham Football club's 'A' team. Lorimer excelled in the 'A' team and he was soon promoted to first-team football. Lorimer made 39 appearances, scoring 99 points in Manningham's 1895/96 Championship success.

On 16 January 1897, although suffering from a heavy cold, Lorimer played in the Manningham v Brighouse Rangers game at Valley Parade. Feeling ill after the game, Lorimer was taken home and diagnosed with acute neuralgia, which soon developed into mild typhoid fever. The Manningham club responded well and appointed a nurse to visit the player. He was later visited by the club doctor Mr Mercer. However, despite some signs of recovery George Lorimer died in the early hours of 8 February 1897 aged just 25 years. His funeral took place at Heaton Baptist Church. Hundreds of mourners walked alongside his horse-drawn hearse and it was estimated that 8,000 people lined the streets from Manningham to Heaton.

John Thomas Toothill. 'Jack' had a distinguished career playing Rugby Union for Manningham and Bradford, gaining caps for both England and Yorkshire. In 1895 the immensely strong and experienced forward decided to join the

Northern Union and made his debut in the new code on the wing in Bradford's inaugural game against Wakefield Trinity. He retired in 1898, his last game for Bradford being the Challenge Cup Final defeat against Batley at Headingley.

A Bramley team pictured around 1896. The club had voted to join the Northern Union at their well-attended 17th annual meeting, on Friday, 29 May 1896. Mr C Akeroyd presided and spoke of a healthy balance sheet and improving results. A resolution in favour of joining the Northern Union was proposed by Mr Johnson Varley and seconded by Mr E Bottom. The resolution was carried with a single member against, who then moved a resolution of loyalty to the English Rugby Union, which was not seconded.

In November 1896 Manningham held a bazaar to raise funds. The bazaar was held, on four consecutive days, in the drill hall of the Belle Vue Barracks on Manningham Lane. The *Bradford Daily Telegraph* publicised the event well and described the scene in the hall: 'The large drill hall has been tastefully arranged as a football field, the goal posts facing each other from the Belle Vue and Lumb Lane ends. A variety of amusements have been provided, including, dramatic, variety, and children's

entertainers, a minstrel troupe and the usual side shows of bran tub, fish pond and living pictures.'

William Anza Cross. 'Billy' was stand-off with the Kendal Hornets club in the mid-1880s. Billy was a gifted player, his grace and skill leading to him being called 'will o' the wisp' by the Kendal supporters. In 1895, with work in Kendal scarce, Billy found a job in St Helens and signed for the town's rugby club. Billy played in Saints' first Northern Union game on 7 September 1895 against Rochdale Hornets and had the distinction of kicking the first goal under Northern Union rules. The Westmerian's style of

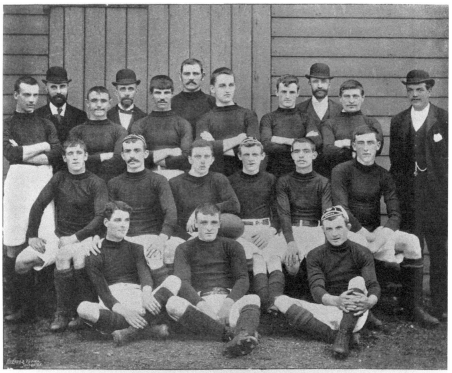

Photograph by R. T. WATSON,   Anlaby Road, Hull.

HULL FOOTBALL CLUB, 1895-96.

H. HILDRITH, (Hon. Sec.)   C. A. BREWER, (President.) G. JACKETTS.   G. W. STEPHENSON, (Hon. Sec.)
H. WILES.   W. MANSELL.   W. HARMER.   J. T. BARKER.   J. TOWNEND.   G. BOOTH.   J. GRAY, (Attendant.)
    E. MAHONEY.   H. THOMPSON.   C. C. LEMPRIERE, (Capt.) C. TOWNEND, (V.-Capt.) W. JOHNSON. A. PLUGGE.
        G. E. BARKER.   W. FEETHAU.   J. HOLMES.

play and great character saw him appointed captain in those early seasons of the new code. Billy made 75 appearances for St Helens, his last in the Challenge Cup third-round tie against Batley at Knowsley Road on 23 March 1901.

Hull FC (opposite bottom), were founder members of the Northern Union and simultaneously played their first home game against Liversedge and opened the club's new home at the Athletic Ground, West Hull, on the 21 September. The city's football supporters were so anxious to witness the new code of football that it was feared that not all the assembled throng would gain admittance. The crowd was estimated to be 8,000, who witnessed a game dominated by the two packs of forwards. In the later stages Hull's three-quarters put together some fine passing movements and a fine series of exchanges between Thompson, Lempriere and Willis prised a gap in the visitors' defence for Jacketts to cross for an unconverted try to give Hull a 3-0 victory. George Jacketts is third from left on the back row.

Like most clubs, Hull FC were very aware that they would need a good financial footing to compete and survive in the new Union and issued member's books, an early form of today's season tickets. This 7/6d booklet is a rare survivor from that very first season.

Jack Hurst of Oldham was one of the stars of Lancashire Rugby Union, a strong wingman blessed with outstanding pace. Hurst was a leading try-scorer and when Oldham became founder members of the Northern Union he continued his prowess on the wing. Hurst was the top try-scorer of the Union's first season with 28 tries. He played his final game for Oldham against Swinton in October 1898. During his brief Northern Union career Hurst scored 62 tries in 80 games.

Runcorn were the first champions of the Lancashire Senior Competition, which, like the Yorkshire competition,

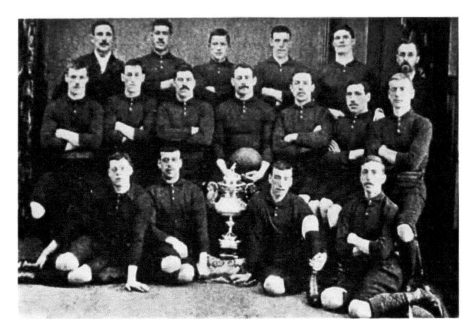

ran alongside the main league. The 'Linnets' had ended the season joint top with Oldham on 28 points from 20 games. Runcorn and Oldham then contested a play-off at Wheater's Field, the home of Broughton Rangers. The game caught the imagination of Lancashire football followers and a crowd of 9,000 paid £174 to witness Runcorn take a 6-0 lead at half-time. Oldham came back with a converted try but Runcorn were crowned champions with a single-point victory.

A Widnes team in 1895/96.

Widnes were founder members of the Northern Union and completed the first season in 16th place.

Back: Joe Acton, Jim Johnson, Fred Hampson, Tom Acton, John Donnelly, Tom Handley aka Hanley, Tom Laws (trainer).

Seated: Charles Emery, Evan Jones, Harry Peters, Dan Brennan, J Hunt, Crane Alford (signed from Aberavon), Bob Baty.

Front: Joe Drummond and William 'Butcher' Rispan.

A Swinton team from the 1896/97 season.

Swinton were one of the leading clubs in the Lancashire Rugby Union and had built a very strong fixture list that attracted huge crowds to their home games at their Chorley Road ground. They had decided in 1895 to stay loyal to the Rugby Union, mainly because of their attractive fixtures which gave the club sound financial stability. However, by 1896 the number of local clubs joining the new Union had reduced Swinton's impressive fixtures and financial position and they were simply struggling. The Lions committee, following meetings with members, players and supporters, decided to apply for membership of the Northern Union. They were accepted into the Union on 7 May 1896. Swinton's leap in the dark began on 5 September 1896 when they entertained founder members Warrington in a Lancashire Senior Competition game at Chorley Road. Witnessed by a crowd of 3,000, the early stages of the game were dominated by the forwards. Eventually the Lions' Westmerian wingman Jonty Goodman broke the deadlock with a superb drop goal. Minutes later Goodman took advantage of a disorganised Warrington defence to gallop over the line for an unconverted try. The Lions' backs were by now playing well and Jim Valentine and Frank Atherton soon crossed for tries. Billy Pearson dropped a goal. Warrington fought back with a penalty goal from Heeson and a try from Lawless to make the result a promising 17-6 victory for Swinton.

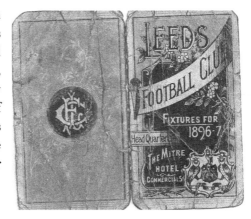

The success of the first season under the Northern Union's control gave clubs a guaranteed and attractive fixture list, compiled by the Union. Many clubs soon took advantage of this by printing fixture booklets like this well designed and rare survivor published by Leeds for the 1896/97 season.

Northern Union clubs were quick to realise that player selection was important to ensure their fixtures took place with a full team of fit and able footballers. The clubs soon took advantage of the postal rates of a halfpenny for postcards introduced in 1894. This surviving Victorian

postcard issued by Leeds Parish Church club in December 1897 gives the player contacted the full details of his selection, the opposition and when and where to meet for travel to the game.

The immensely experienced administrator David Fox Burnley was elected President of the Yorkshire Senior Competition for season 1896/97 and vice-chairman of the Northern Union in 1897/98. His skills led to him being elected chairman of the Northern Union in 1898/99. David Burnley served on the Batley committee from 1880 until his death in 1910. He was the club's financial secretary from 1880 to 1883 and then president/chairman from 1883 to 1899.

BRIGHOUSE RANGERS' F.C.

Spring Bank, Brighouse,
Oct. 13th, 1897.

Dear Sir,—

The following is the team selected to represent the Club in the Competition match versus Liversedge, at Lane Head, on Saturday:—

H. Jones, back; B. Holroyd, L. Brooke, W. Nichol (junior), and A. Beaumont, three-quarter backs; L. Ross and E. England, half backs; A. G. Sugden, E. Ayrton, W. Nichol, F. Wood, E. Croft, S. Priestley, T. Armitage, and R. E. Sugden (capt.), forwards.

Players are requested to be on the ground at 2-45. Kick-off at 3-30.

The second team will leave the Stag and Pheasant at 2 o'clock by waggonette.

If you are unable to play from any cause whatever kindly communicate with Mr. Kilner immediately.

PLAYERS' MEETINGS:—
FIRST TEAM, THURSDAY EVENING, at 7-30.
SECOND TEAM, FRIDAY EVENING, at 7-30.

Yours truly,

GEO. KILNER, } Secs.
J. HOLLIDAY,

Brighouse Rangers used a different system of contacting their players for selection – a quite formal letter with all selected payers named instead of a simple postcard to individual players. It is not known if this item was actually posted to players or displayed in a clubhouse or public house used as the club's headquarters.

A. Field
Captain, Rochdale Hornets F.C., who distinguished himself in the recent county match Lancs v. Yorks.

A rare season-ticket booklet issued by Wakefield Trinity for the 1896/97 season.

Archie Field was a gifted and well-respected Rugby Union footballer in the Northampton area in the early 1890s. In 1898 he decided to move north and signed for Rochdale Hornets, making his debut in December 1898. Field settled well into Northern Union football and soon became a favourite of the Rochdale supporters. A dispute with the Rochdale committee in 1900 led to Field returning to his home town of Olney. However, Hornets somehow managed to bring him back to Rochdale in 1901, where he played until his retirement and return to Olney. On his return to Northamptonshire he joined the Oxford and Bucks light infantry and died of wounds in hospital in France.

Tom Pook was born in Plymouth and played Rugby Union for Welsh first-class club Newport. Although at 5ft 6in he was quite short for a forward, he had great pace. He represented Wales against Scotland in Edinburgh in January 1895. In 1898 he decided to move north and made his debut for the Holbeck Northern Union club on 3 September 1898. Holbeck played Birkenhead Wanderers in the Challenge Cup first round in 1899. The Welshman must have seen something he liked about the club because Pook moved to Birkenhead Wanderers in late 1900 and his vast experience led to him assisting with the coaching there.

A surviving member's season-ticket book from the Hunslet club for 1897/98 season. The booklets were well printed with strong covers and perforated pages, which eased congestion at designated members' turnstiles.

In 1895 the Heckmondwike Old Athletic club witnessed their Rugby Union fixture list decimated when the Northern Union was formed. In April 1896 players, officials and supporters of the club held a meeting to discuss their predicament. Mr J Atkin presided and moved that the club apply for permission to join the Northern Union. He added that if the proposals were passed it would be certain that admission would be granted and Heckmondwike would be one of the 16 that would form the Yorkshire Senior Competition. Mr Harvey Spivey seconded and after a brief discussion the motion was carried unanimously. Heckmondwike were accepted into the new Union and on 11 September 1897 they played their first Northern Union football game at their Beck Lane ground. Lee scored a try in a 3-2 victory over Bramley.

Heckmondwike's membership of the Northern Union became one of constant struggle. Their poor results led to very poor gates. Competing in the

W. HOLLINWOOD.   H. HALLIDAY.   J. WELSH.
W. GILLGALLON.
J. A. FIRTH.   D. GOUGH.   C. WALFORD. A. KNOWLES.   D. JOWETT.   J. JACKSON.

Photo by J. Wood.   Heckmondwike.
C. JACKSON.   J. LOCKWOOD.   G. HARRISON.   W. GILDEA.   J. COLEMAN.
HECKMONDWIKE.

Yorkshire Senior Competition, in their first three seasons from 1896/97 to 1898/99 the club were victors in only 16 games. The 'Lane Enders' hit rock bottom when they ended the 1898/99 season at the foot of the league table. On 21 April 1899 the club opposed Hull Kingston Rovers, the champions of the Yorkshire Senior Competition Second Division, in a promotion/ relegation test match at Clarence Field, the home of Leeds Parish Church. It was estimated that a crowd of 7,000 witnessed the Rovers trounce Heckmondwike 21-3 to give them promotion and plunge Heckmondwike into the depths of obscurity in the Second Division. In 1901/02 14 clubs held a series of secret meetings and broke from the Northern Union competitions to form a Northern Rugby League. The breakaway greatly reduced the Lancashire and Yorkshire Senior Competitions and several clubs from the Second Division were invited to join the senior leagues. Heckmondwike, having somehow survived the Second Division wilderness, were promoted to the senior competition. The form of the 'Lane Enders' in the Challenge Cup that season was simply incredible. They defeated Birkenhead Wanderers 5-0 in the first round and went on to beat Holbeck 7-5, then continued the run with a 7-4 victory over Ossett. The fourth-round draw favoured Heckmondwike with another home tie, this time against Hunslet and their mighty forwards. The home side held the Parksiders to a 2-2 draw. The following Wednesday Hunslet brought Heckmondwike's much-welcomed days of glory to an end with a 6-2 victory. The league season was the usual disappointment for the Beck Lane club, and after finishing in 11th position they resigned from the Northern Union and formed an Association Football Club. The photograph is from 1897.

In 1897 the Northern Union had a dilemma. The actions, although principled, of the original 22 clubs that had formed the Union had created chaos in Lancashire and Yorkshire, when many of the leading clubs who had stayed with the Rugby Union witnessed their fixtures reduced when clubs broke away to the Northern Union. There was a surge in new members from clubs who had little interest in broken-time payments but just wanted a decent fixture list to provide adequate 'gates' to allow them to keep going.

The Union's solution was to abandon the cumbersome single league and to form two regional leagues, the Lancashire and Yorkshire Senior Competitions.

The 1897/98 Yorkshire Senior Competition ended with Hunslet and Bradford tied at the top of the league table with 48 points each. The competition committee decided that a play-off game would be held to decide the champions. On 30 April 1898 Hunslet defeated Bradford 5-2

HUNSLET FOOTBALL TEAM.

to be crowned champions, Ramage scoring a try and Albert Goldthorpe kicked a goal. F W Cooper scored Bradford's points with a goal. It is not known where this photograph was taken. Albert Goldthorpe, Hunslet's captain, is holding the Championship shield.

Frank Harry joined Broughton Rangers in September 1899.

His route to Broughton was intriguing. Born in Devon in 1876, he developed into a fine rugby footballer and soon signed for Torquay Athletic RFU club where he excelled at full back. However, in November 1898 his career took a strange turn when the English RFU suspended Torquay. The ERU had received information from the Welsh RFU of an attempt, by an alleged emissary of Torquay, to secure the services of McConnell of the Cardiff St Peter's club by offering inducements of a job and sums of money for playing. Frank Harry was cited by the ERU as the instigator, and although the Devon's club suspension was lifted Harry was soon suspended. The case against him hinged on the letter sent to Cardiff. Harry denied writing the letter, explaining that the letter had been written by his wife, who had used the football club's headed notepaper. He also refused to hand the documents over, saying they were

private. His suspension was not lifted.

In early September 1899 Harry left Devon to join Broughton Rangers. He made his debut at full back on 7 October in Rangers' away defeat at Stockport. Frank Harry was also a gifted cricketer, scoring 1,605 runs and taking 215 wickets for Lancashire from 1903 to 1908. He had brief spells with Worcestershire and Durham during World War One. He retired in 1920 and then stood as umpire for 21 games in 1921. He died in 1925 in Great Malvern.

A contemporary sketch of Stockport's

Fred Saville kicking a first-half goal for Cheshire during the Yorkshire v Cheshire County Championship game at Valley Parade, Manningham, on 29 October 1898. 'Old Ebor's' match report in the *Bradford Daily Observer* described the conditions: 'In

thick muggy weather the mist lay deep in the valley, but in the absence of rain, conditions were relatively pleasant.' He described Saville's penalty goal as 'the best seen at Valley Parade for many a season.'

In the second half Yorkshire took control of the game and tries from Lumley (Leeds) Sutcliffe (Huddersfield) and a brace from Rigg (Halifax) and a goal from Albert Goldthorpe (Hunslet) gave them a 14-2 victory. Lancashire won the County Championship.

The Holbeck squad outside the Waggon and Horses, their headquarters, in 1900.

Holbeck joined the Northern Union in May 1896. The 'Imps' played at the Recreation Ground, which was situated on land between the existing Top Moor side and Brown Lane. In January Holbeck raised £2,000 with a share issue and became a limited company to buy a piece of land on Elland Road owned by Bentley's Yorkshire Breweries. The money spent on

HOLBECK.

Photo by Wm. Harrison, Meadow Road.

TERRY (*Trainer*).   DAVIS.   DORAN.   LANG. HOYLE. JOLLIFFE. WILKINSON.
McCARTHY.   HAWKINS. BUCKLER (*Capt.*) HAINSTOCK. HEXTER. STEAD.
O'BRIEN.   HIRST.   POOK.   HEMSLEY.

creating the new ground drained the club's finances and, unable to attract new players, Holbeck struggled in the new Union. In the 1903/04 campaign the 'Imps' finished joint-second with St Helens in the Rugby League Second Division. On 14 May 1904 Holbeck lost their chance of promotion when they were beaten 7-0 by St Helens in the promotion play-off at Fartown, Huddersfield. The defeat and subsequent relegation was a huge blow. Support had dwindled and many of their players had left for bigger clubs and far better terms. A major loss to the Imps was Tom Pook, the Welsh RFU international forward, who joined Birkenhead Wanderers shortly after Holbeck had played the Wanderers in the Challenge Cup. Off the field, Holbeck were victims of the rise of Association Football in Leeds when in August 1904 they lost their New Peacock ground to the new Association Football club Leeds City, which had been formed from the remnants of the highly successful Hunslet FC, who had been offered the ground by the company directors of the Holbeck ground.

The Holbeck club were very wary of playing another season in the Second Division with a poor squad, small gates and very little money. They decided to fold and resigned from the Union.

Brighouse Rangers, 1897.
Brighouse Rangers were formed in the 1870s and were founder members of the Northern Union. The Rangers established a ground on Waterloo Road,

WILKINSON.   B. NAYLOR.   J. HEAP.   W. NICHOLL. M. TAYLOR.
G. KILNER.   F. WOOD. EARNSHAW. T. H. HUGHES. F. KEIR.
W. JAGGAR.   ABBEY.   R. E. SUGDEN.   ENGLAND.
BEAUMONT.   ROSS.   WHITELEY.   SUGDEN.

Photo by J. Wood.   Brighouse.
HARTLEY.   L. BROOKE.   BOOTHMAN.
BRIGHOUSE RANGERS.

Lane End and soon developed into a strong and capable Rugby Union side, culminating in 1895 when they opposed Morley in the Yorkshire Rugby Union Cup Final. 20,000 football supporters gathered at Headingley to witness Brighouse defeat Morley 16-4 and bring 'T'owd Tin Pot' back to the Royal Hotel, the Rangers headquarters at the time. In August 1895 Brighouse attended the meeting at the George Hotel, Huddersfield, and became one of the clubs that formed the Northern Union. The club's long-standing chairman Harry Waller was elected the Union's first president.

The competence Brighouse had revealed in their final season playing Rugby Union was soon apparent in the new code of football, and by the season's end they finished in fifth position. The following season, 1896/97, the Northern Union abandoned the one-league system and formed two county competitions. Brighouse were crowned champions of the Yorkshire Senior Competition. Unfortunately, Brighouse then began a slump in fortunes and in late August 1906 the club, badly short of money to continue, folded and resigned from the Northern Union. At the time of their demise it was suggested that the Brighouse Cricket and Bowling Club should install a football branch and extend its ground, thus providing both winter and summer pastimes at one centre. The idea was not taken up.

The Mighty Bongers: Tyldesley's side of 1895 lines up six years before going defunct *Mike Latham*

Tyldesley, pictured in 1895/96, were founder members of the Northern Union. The club was formed c.1879 and played at a ground near Garrett Hall. Two years later they moved to a field near to their headquarters on Sale Lane. In 1886 the ambitious club moved to a ground at Well Street where they acquired the nickname 'The Mighty Bongers.' In 1888 the 'bongers' signed John 'Buff' Berry, far right on the photograph, from Kendal Hornets. With 'Buff' at half back, Tyldesley became a major force in the seasons prior to the split. In 1896 the 'Bongers' finished their first season in the Northern Union in a creditable sixth place. Unfortunately, Tyldesley soon found they were basically a small club from a small town and were unable to compete with the bigger clubs. They eventually found themselves in the 1900/01 Second Division of the Lancashire Senior Competition, a forgotten league with disastrously little or no support from the Northern Union. Tyldesley survived just one season and played their last match at home to Birkenhead Wanderers on 6 April 1901, witnessed by 400 people. Four days later the club folded and their assets, including hoardings, turnstiles and grandstands, were sold at auction for a miserable £30.

On 29 August 1895 the Stockport Rugby Union Club, pictured here in the 1898/99 Northern Union season, were unable to send a representative to the meeting at the George Hotel, Huddersfield. However, determined to break away from the RFU, the committee telegraphed the meeting asking to be included in the breakaway Union. The Union's committee accepted Stockport's request and they became members of the Northern Union. Stockport's first match at their Edgeley Park ground in the brave new world was a home defeat by Brighouse Rangers. A crowd of around 5,000 witnessed the fixture against the Yorkshire Rugby Union Cup holders, and despite the loss the afternoon was declared a great success. Stockport struggled on in the Northern Union, but the rise of Association Football in the town hit Stockport's gates. In 1902 Stockport County AFC moved in to Edgeley Park, a ground share to ostensibly help prevent it from being purchased by a brewery. Stockport ended the 1902/03 season at the bottom of the league, and in early August 1903 the club folded and County took over the ground. The continual rise of the 'dribbling game' had claimed another scalp in the war to establish a new code of football.

A rare photograph of a game at Edgeley Park, Stockport, around 1900.

The Leeds Parish Church football team squad, pictured during the 1898/99 NU Yorkshire Senior Competition season. The football team was formed around 1874 to 1879 as part of the church recreation section, an attempt to bring the Muscular Christianity movement to the working class of

LEEDS PARISH CHURCH.

Photo by Harrison, Meadow Road.

G. GREENWOOD.   CLEGG. GREENWOOD.
ODDY.   DEWS. MCNICHOLAS. CROMPTON. DAVIDSON. WADE.   LEWIS.   MOSLEY.
HEWLETT. WAINRIGHT. KNIGHT. LOUGHLIN. CORCORAN, FAWCETT. SMITH. CLAYTON. LEACH (*Trainer,*).
(*Capt.*)

Leeds. The association was a philosophical group that originated in England in the mid-19th century, characterised by a belief in patriotic duty, manliness, the moral and physical beauty of athleticism, teamwork, discipline, self-sacrifice and the expulsion of all that is effeminate, un-English and excessively intellectual. The good intentions of the movement were largely ignored by the members of Leeds Parish Church FC when they soon developed into a club that, allegedly, used illegal payments and inducements to strengthen their team and certainly employed excessive rough and dirty tactics during games. They played their home games at Clarence Field, Crown Point, a ground over Crown Point bridge that led to the club's nickname 'T' lads from over t' bridge'. The ground was very near to the Leyland's district of the city, an area predominantly populated by Jewish immigrants. The youths of the quarter soon took to attending home games to try to integrate with Leeds life. Leeds Parish Church were accepted into the Northern Union in 1896 and joined the Yorkshire Senior Competition, where they were to stay throughout their membership of the union. They developed into a mediocre club in the league competition. In 1900 they were fined £20 when a section of their passionate supporters attacked the Brighouse Rangers team by throwing a series of missiles at them. Rawlinson of Brighouse was hit on the nose by an iron nut one and a half inches thick and weighing 8.5 ounces, and another player, Denham, was injured by a piece of hard cinder.

In the 1899/00 season the Churchmen embarked on an incredible run of victories in the Challenge Cup Competition. They defeated Seaton 5-0, then Altrincham 15-3. In the third round, twice winners of the cup, Batley were vanquished 7-2. A crowd of 20,000 witnessed Parish Church draw 5-5 with Runcorn in the quarter-final at Clarence Field. The Churchmen defeated Runcorn 8-6 in the replay to set up a semi-final against Swinton at Oldham. The mighty Lions of Swinton were just too strong for Parish Church and, witnessed by 14,000 at the Watersheddings ground, won the game 8-0. Swinton went on to defeat rivals Salford 16-8 in the final at Fallowfield, Manchester.

In July 1901 the Leeds Parish Church FC resigned from the Northern Union due to problems with the lease of their ground.

The Castleford Northern Union club c.1900. The Castleford RFU club was formed around 1877 and were based at a ground on Lock Lane. They gradually grew into a successful team, producing many internationals. In 1896 Castleford defeated the Leeds-based West Riding club in the final of the Yorkshire Challenge Cup. A crowd of 10,000 witnessed

Photo by Walker & Co.

A. W. WADE, WEBSTER. DOOLEY. WALTON. HEPTINSTALL. WARD. CHURCH. SALMONI. F. MARTON,
(Chairman). NEIL. DUNN. HOLLAND. SPEED. TOWNEND. CARTER. (Com.)
SMART. BRADY.

Castleford's 3-0 victory at Morley's Scatcherd Lane ground. However, Castleford were soon to become a club in turmoil. Castleford, like many Yorkshire RFU clubs, had suffered when the 1895 split seriously affected their fixtures and income. In May 1896 the club met to discuss the possible advantages of joining the Northern Union. At a packed meeting the proposal to leave the RFU and join the NU was defeated by 99 votes to 40. However, Northern Union supporters were determined to move the club forward and on 12 May arranged a meeting at the George and Dragon Hotel. Mr Job Harling chaired the meeting, attended by around 90 people, and gave a passionate speech setting out the advantages to the town and tradespeople that membership of the Northern Union would bring. Mr A. W. Wade proposed that a new club be formed to be called the Castleford FC and that they join the Northern Union. The proposal was carried, and the club was accepted into the Yorkshire Senior Competition. The new club soon created a ground at the opposite side of Lock Lane, some 200 yards away from the Rugby Union ground. The club worked hard draining and levelling the pitch then erecting two stands 50 yards long and able to accommodate 2,000 spectators. The ground soon became known as Sandy Desert. The creation of a Northern Union club in the town soon became popular and 2,000 attended a trial match played under NU rules.

Castleford finished their first season in the 1896/97 Yorkshire Senior Competition in sixth place and the club soon developed into a mid-table league side. In 1901 Castleford greatly improved their modest league form and shocked the Northern Union when they had a tremendous run of success in the Challenge Cup Competition. In the first round they held Manningham to a 0-0 draw at Valley Parade and then trounced them 21-2 at home. They went on to beat Workington 3-2 and then defeated Dewsbury 5-3 at Crown Flatt. In the quarter-final Castleford held Hull Kingston Rovers 5-5 at Hull, then overcome the Rovers 7-2 back home in Castleford. The club ventured into the unknown when they faced Warrington in the semi-final. Castleford were basically outclassed by Warrington and were overwhelmed 21-5 in the game at Wheater's Field, Broughton. Castleford stuck to their old-fashioned forward play methods and as one eye-witness account recorded:

'The severe drubbing was inflicted by the Warrington backs of whom Dickenson, Isherwood and Fish simply toyed with the opposing three-quarters. Smith and Salmoni played well for Castleford in an individual sense, but on the losing side there was no combination worth mentioning.'

By 1906 the club was deeply in debt and, struggling to pay the players, took the only action available and folded.

THE NATURAL DEVELOPMENT OF A FOOTBALLER.

In 1899 the *Bradford Daily Telegraph* published this cartoon of a footballer depicted as a publican. The Bradford club had six players who were publicans, including Jimmy Wright, Jack Toothill, Joe Richards and Tom Broadley. Manningham had nine publicans including Fred Clegg, Rob Poocock, Johnny Bramham and Alf Leach.

The Bradford winger and champion sprinter F. W. Cooper joined the list of the city's publican players in March 1899 when he took control of the Parkside Hotel. He soon advertised his presence and his magnificent display of trophies, and sparkling ales and fine wines.

A very scarce teamsheet for the Hull v Leeds Parish Church match on 21 January 1899. Such ephemeral items are rare survivors of the late-

HULL v. LEEDS PARISH CHURCH.

Corrected by Telegram this morning.

HULL—	LEEDS PARISH CHURCH—
Back—G. Sillis.	*Back*—Corcoran.
Three-quarter backs—C. C. Lempriere, W. Jacques, T. Savage and W. Hodgson.	*Three-quarter backs*—Fawcett, Lewis, Knight and Smith.
Half-backs-D. Frank & J. Thompson.	*Half-back*—Mosley and Langheur.
Forwards—H. Wiles (capt.), W. Dale, G. Voyce, R. Rhodes, F. Gorman, R. Forshaw, J. H. Rippon and G. Jacketts.	*Forwards*—Wainwright, Thackray, Clayton, Hewlett, Davison, McNicholas, Tolcan and Walker.
Referee—Mr. Rowlands.	*Touch Judges*—Messrs. Depledge and Sewell.

TO-DAY'S SCORES.

	Goals	Tries	Points		Goals	Tries	Points
Hull				L. P. Church			

Victorian era. The Yorkshire Senior Competition fixture attracted a crowd of 12,000, including an estimated 1,000 from Leeds, despite the severe weather conditions. The Churchmen started well, and their hefty pack soon launched a series of strong raids into the Hull half, the class of the home side's backs soon told when Lempriere launched a superb cross-kick to enable Voyce to score an unconverted try. Hull took control of the game and Jacques soon scored a try in the corner. The Churchmen's forwards second-half play was once again exceptional, but their backs let them down. The home backs soon took control and a fine run by Hodgson, who intercepted a pass, ended in Wiles scoring and Jacques adding a goal. Minutes later Forshaw burst over for an unconverted try. The result was at times a hard fought 14-0 victory for the home side. Hull ended the season in seventh place and the Churchmen in 14th.

The Lancashire XV that played Cumberland in the NU County Championship game at Watersheddings, Oldham, on 21 October 1899. The 8,000 attendance must have been enhanced by the fact that the Lancashire team had six Oldham players in its ranks. In a close game Cumberland came to within two points, until late tries by Davies and Hadwen and a goal from Frater gave the Lancastrians a 17-7 victory.

The players are (left to right) Aspey, Frater, Harrison, Morrison, Tunney. (Middle) Kruger, Briers, Lawton, Davies, Williams. (Front) Fletcher, Hadwen, Thomas, Taylor and Vigsey.

Lancashire were crowned County Champions that season, winning all three of their games.

Crowds at Northern Union games could be very passionate in their support of their local team as this evocative late-Victorian cartoon illustrates very well. Referee-baiting was almost obligatory at many grounds. Unfortunately, often good-humoured vocal banter occasionally led to random acts of civil disturbance. Crowds at Rochdale were often guilty of violence, and in February 1896 the Hornet's Athletic Grounds was closed

THE CROWD FROM THE REFEREES POINT OF VIEW.

for six weeks when the referee was attacked after a game. In November of the same year sections of the Rochdale crowd attacked the opposition team and the ground was closed for five weeks. In December 1897 'rowdy conduct' by boys at Rochdale was given a different form of punishment when 200 notices were displayed in the town and boys' admission prices were increased to 6d. One incident which went unpunished occurred in January 1897 at Park Avenue, Bradford, when the referee was pelted with snowballs. However, a youth was arrested at Huddersfield for throwing a knife onto the pitch. The Northern Union formed a sub-committee in 1897 to investigate the problems, and after considering their report issued the following instructions to all clubs:

'All club committees must warn players regarding rough play and their attitude to referees.

Post warning notices on the ground, send a circular to members re bad conduct by spectators.'

The disturbances continued when the referee was attacked by the recidivists in the crowd at Rochdale and at Dewsbury, Runcorn, Huddersfield and Keighley.

Lancaster Northern Union club with the North West Challenge Cup at their Quay Meadow ground around 1900. The players' names are not known, although it is believed the captain, holding the ball, is John Pinch. The club was one of many which joined the Northern Union in 1896/97. Like many of the new arrivals, Lancaster suffered in the new U nion. The lack of planning and organisation from the Northern Union gave them little chance to succeed or even survive. Initially they were members of the Lancashire Senior Competition and then in 1905 the ill-fated new single league was formed when the Northern Union adopted a laissez-faire attitude by insisting clubs arranged their own fixtures. For Lancaster the system merely

accelerated their demise. Clubs were reluctant to incur the costs to travel to the far north of Lancashire for an unattractive fixture with Lancaster. In June 1905 the club, with debts of over £100, went out of business, another needless casualty of a Union struggling to control the ambitions of the big clubs and to organise a league system that would help junior clubs thrive and survive.

York, winners of the Yorkshire Senior Competition Eastern Section in the 1900/01 season. The club was formed in 1868 by former pupils of St

The York Football Team. Season 1900-1.
Winners of the East Division Second Competition.

Peter's School and soon became known as 'the Wasps' because of their distinctive amber-and-black hooped shirts. York found it difficult to find a permanent ground in the cramped city and solved the problem by using a pair of portable posts to erect at any suitable field they could find. They played several games on the historic Knavesmire, now the York racecourse, before moving to the York Gentlemen's cricket ground, Wigginton Road, in the early 1880s. In 1883 the nomadic club was on the move again when a merger with York Melbourne brought a move to Poad's fields, Fulford Road. York joined the Northern Union in April 1898 and played their games at Clarence Street, their home until March 1989. The Wasps thrived and survived the infamous Yorkshire Second Competition and were champions of the Eastern Section. York defeated Heckmondwike, the Western Section champions, in a play-off and then had to play Liversedge, the bottom club in the Yorkshire Senior Competition, in the promotion /relegation final.

The teams met at Hunslet's Parkside ground on 20 April, where a good crowd of 6,000 witnessed a 0-0 draw. The replay at Belle Vue, Wakefield, attracted 2,000 spectators and a poor gate of £37. The next day the teams met again, with the Northern Union stipulating that should the game be undecided following 80 minutes' play extra time of two halves of 15 minutes each way would be played. At the Leeds Parish Church's ground York finally gained promotion to the Yorkshire Senior Competition when they defeated Liversedge 10-0.

Leeds's squad for the 1899/1900 season. The club's fifth season in the Northern Union was an eventful one. The committee were having

problems in building a strong, reliable squad and during the season 21 new players were introduced to football at Headingley. To make matters worse, in January 1900 five regular first-team players refused to play in the game against Batley unless their demands for better conditions were met. The Leeds committee, which had recently made increases in payments, met with the strikers and stated that the committee, not the players, made the decisions and their demands would not be met. The players involved, Rogan, Gregg, G. Glover and W. Glover, were all suspended for a month. In March, Rogan, who Leeds believed was the ring leader, was reported to the league for insubordination. The Yorkshire Senior Competition committee promptly suspended Rogan sine die. The squad was by now far from settled and were still in danger of relegation until a fortunate run of four victories late in the season saved them. However, Leeds ended the season in 15th place with just 17 points, and way behind their rivals in the city. Any thoughts of a successful Challenge Cup campaign ended in the first round when they were defeated 5-0 by junior club Normanton.

A Warrington side at Barrow in January 1900. Warrington had sent a strong team for the Lancashire Senior Competition fixture at Barrow's Cavendish Park and were firm favourites to beat the Furness-based club. From the kick-off the visitors soon displayed their class. Jack Fish, the club's star wingman, burst through an opening in the Barrow defence and sprinted half the length of the field only to be held just short of the line. Within minutes Fish crossed the line in the corner for an unconverted try. The home side soon took control of the game and their forwards

gained most of the possession from the scrums. The Barrow backs took full advantage of their forwards' hard work and astonished the crowd of 3,000 and the visitors. With a bewildering display of passing movements that soon led to tries for Bamber and Bowden and a half-time advantage. Barrow continued to dominate in the second half and were 14-5 victors.

Thomas Hyde Dobson. 'Tommy' was a gifted sprinter and RFU centre. He began his rugby career with local Bradford clubs Undercliffe, Laisterdyke and Bowling. His pace and try-scoring feats soon caught the attention of Bradford FC and he was drafted into the back division of the Park Avenue-based club around 1892. Dobson converted to Northern Union football and in 1895/96 overtook F.W. Cooper's try-scoring record.

In November 1902 Tommy was taken ill after eating raw mussels in a Bradford pub. A doctor was called for but his condition soon became worse. Another doctor attended and pronounced him beyond human aid. Tommy Dobson died in the early hours of 12 November 1902, his cause of death recorded as blood poisoning.

Chapter 2

RESIGNATIONS AND REVIVAL
1901 TO 1909

A cartoon published in January 1901 on the front page of the Manchester-based *Athletic News* depicts the dominant industries in the Lancashire towns of Swinton (coal) and Oldham (cotton) to illustrate the intense rivalry in the race for the Lancashire Senior Competition trophy. Both clubs had strong ambitions to be league champions and met at the Watersheddings, the home of Oldham, in

THE RACE FOR THE LANCASHIRE CUP.

COAL CONQUERS COTTON.

early January. Interest in the game was exceptional and special trains of supporters began leaving Swinton at ten in the morning. The ground was inundated by fans long before noon and the massive crush prompted the Oldham club officials to lock the gates over an hour before the kick-off. Inside the ground spectators had begun to encroach onto the field of play and this increased when the teams took to the field. Swinton's captain Jim Valentine appealed to the referee to abandon the game. However, the game went on and a hard-fought contest ended with a 7-5 victory to Swinton. Both clubs lodged protests to the LSC committee who, following a three-hour meeting, declared the game should be replayed the following Wednesday. On the Tuesday before the game Queen Victoria died and as a mark of respect the game was postponed. The next scheduled replay was also postponed when referee Frank Renton of Hunslet declared the frozen Watersheddings pitch unplayable. The clubs did eventually contest the game, a 3-3 draw. Oldham's well-earned point that afternoon eventually led to the club being crowned champions of the Lancashire Senior Competition.

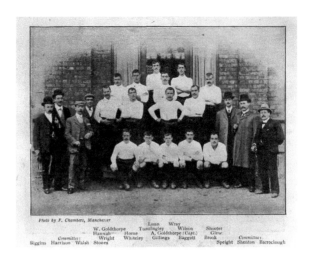

Lunn   Wray
W. Goldthorpe   Tuntingley   Wilson   Shooter
Hannah   Horne   A. Goldthorpe (Capt.)   Glew
Committee: Wright   Whiteley   Gillings   Baggott   Brook   Committee:
Biggins Harrison Walsh Stones   Speight Shenton Barroclough

The Hunslet squad from 1901, the 'Parksiders', ended their Yorkshire Senior Competition campaign in third position. Their celebrated captain Albert Goldthorpe (second right, middle row) kicked 44 goals during the season and Lunn (left on the back row) made three appearances for the Yorkshire Ccounty team. The Hunslet club were busy recruiting new players to replace their older squad members. Hunslet were great believers in a strong pack of forwards and that season signed two promising front rowers, Walter Wray (right on the back row) from Methley Parish Church and Bill 'Tubby' Brooke (far right, front row) from Kippax. Both players had long careers with Hunslet, Brooke making 306 appearances up to his retirement in 1910 and Wray 221 appearances up to his transfer to York in 1908.

Kendal Hornets squad pictured with the Westmorland and North West Lancashire Cup and medals in 1902. Kendal was a famous centre for the handling code in the late-Victorian era. The Westmorland market town had two major clubs, the Hornets, formed in 1871, and Town, formed in 1884,

following a merger between the Albion and Excelsior clubs. The intense rivalry and the expansive style of play of games between the Hornets and Town soon attracted the scouts from the big clubs of the Lancashire and Yorkshire leagues. Both clubs suffered from valuable players moving south, especially the Hornets, who lost their star half backs 'Buff' Berry to Tyldesley and Billy Cross to St Helens. With the loss of many good players, football in Kendal rapidly declined and Kendal Town folded in 1894 and the Hornets in 1896. However, in 1898 a reformed Kendal Hornets were accepted into the Northern Union, eventually taking part in the Lancashire Senior Competition Second Division in 1900. The club soon realised joining the league with the unaffordable travelling costs was a mistake and withdrew to play in the local leagues. The club eventually folded in April 1904.

Fred Webster was one of the great forwards of the Edwardian era of Northern Union football. Born in 1882 in Thorne, Webster was signed by Leeds from the Brotherton junior club on the eve of his 20th birthday. He made his debut for Leeds in the game against Dewsbury at Crown Flatt on 13 September 1902. Webster soon settled into the higher standard of football played at Leeds and became one of club's finest players. Webster's skills soon caught the attention of the county selectors and Webster gained Yorkshire representative honours. In 1910 he was selected to be a member of the first squad of Northern Union players to tour Australia and New Zealand. Fred excelled on the tour and made 14 appearances, scoring three tries. On his return to Yorkshire he

was appointed captain of the Leeds club and in 1913 created a club record when he scored eight tries in the club's 102-0 victory over Coventry. Fred Webster played for Leeds for 18 years, making 543 appearances, scoring 76 tries and kicking four goals.

Maryport with the Cumberland Senior Competition cup at Netherhall in 1903. Maryport opposed Seaton in the final on their own ground. The home side kicked off against a strong wind. Play in the first half was fast and evenly contested in midfield, but eventually Maryport's forwards gained the advantage, only to be let down with a series of wild passes going to ground.

Finally, Robley gained possession from a kick and dribbled over the Seaton line for an unconverted try. In the second half the home side took control and Smith, Timoney and Dixon scored tries, all converted by Robley, and Maryport were well deserved 18-0 winners. The trophy was presented by Miss Senhouse and afterwards the players drove around the town followed by a tremendous crowd of cheering people.

Early photographs of Northern Union matches are scarce. Photographers knew the limits of their basic equipment and tended to capture images of teams and individual players. This rare image believed to date from 1903

records action in a game between Hull FC and Hunslet at the Boulevard. An unknown Hunslet player in white moves to attempt a tackle on a Hull player.

Bradford with the Northern Union Championship trophy in 1904. Prior to the split in 1895, Bradford had been one of the leading RFU clubs in the north of England and had built an impressive fixture list opposing the foremost Welsh and southern clubs. The club's forward-dominated style of play was successful in the early seasons of Northern Union football, and by the 1903/04 season Bradford had introduced a very capable back division that augmented the forwards to create a well-balanced side. The race for the 1903/04 Championship was a keenly-fought competition between Salford and Bradford, which was continuously in the balance. Bradford had defeated Salford 9-0 at Park Avenue in December. However, in late March

Photo by R. Scott.   **BRADFORD   F.C.**   Copyright, J.B., L.
                    Bobson, trainer   Sinton   Nessiling   Sharratt
          Hutt   Barker   Greenwood   Smales   Feather   Mosby   Eagers
                    Dunbavin   Gunn   Rees   Marsden, capt.   Turner   Laidlow   Deckan
                                    Surman   Drew

Salford defeated the Bradfordians 4-2 in a tense encounter at The Willows, a victory which put Salford two points above Bradford. The Park Avenue men recovered and beat Keighley, Batley and Hunslet, which left the final league fixture of the season against Broughton Rangers at Park Avenue. The Bradford men understood they needed to win and reverted to their old methods of strong forward play, and led by Tom Broadley launched a series rushing and dribbling movements into Broughton's defence. Although described as a poor game, Bradford were 5-0 victors and ended the season in joint-first position with Salford. The Northern Union arranged a play-off game at Hanson Lane, Halifax, on Thursday 28 April to decide the champions. Interest in the game was great and a crowd of 12,000 braved the wet weather to witness the encounter. Play was evenly contested in the first half and then in the second half Bradford's wing man Mosby kicked a penalty goal. Salford responded well and were soon attacking until Dechan collected a loose ball and passed to George Marsden, who sprinted forward to set up a fine passing movement which resulted in Hutt scoring a try. In the final minutes of the game Bradford defended well and were 5-0 victors and champions. A huge crowd had gathered at the Exchange Station to welcome the champions back home and escort them to their Park Avenue home.

The Leeds squad for 1903/04 pictured at their Headingley home. Players only (back row) Mosley, Davies, Evans, Woolf. Third row: Taylor, Ward, Moon,

Leeds 1903/4

Moffatt. Seated: Stead, Webster, Littlewood, Grace, Dean, Llewellyn, Jenkins. Front row: Hewlett, Birch, Crumpton. Leeds ended the season in sixth place in the First Division of the Northern Rugby League with 43 points. In the Challenge Cup the club defeated Hull Kingston Rovers 3-2 at Craven Street, East Hull, then defeated Keighley 13-0 at Headingley. A third-round visit to Thrum Hall, Halifax, ended the Loiner's cup run when the cup holders, and eventual winners, Halifax beat them 8-2. Littlewood was the top scorer with 25 goals.

The Leeds club endorse Zam Buk in a well-designed, full-page advert from January 1904. Zam Buk was a patent antiseptic herbal balm invented in Australia by Charles Edward Fulford. In 1900 Fulford's older brother

Frank Harris Fulford moved to Leeds to set up the company's expansion into England. He became the managing director following his brother's sudden death and in 1902 opened a factory in Carlton Street, Woodhouse, where they also produced bile beans. The Fulfords were early pioneers of aggressive marketing and soon realised the potential of selling Zam Buk to the many footballers in Leeds and the north of England and advertised heavily in the local newspapers, often using individuals to recommend their product.

At the opening of the 1902/03 season the finances of the Manningham Northern Union Club were in a perilous state. The once powerful club and first champions of the Northern Union were struggling. The proud Bradfordians were reluctant to ask the Northern Union for help and instead devised a New Year's Day fundraising carnival at their Valley Parade ground. The committee organised a friendly football match with Leeds and also a harrier's race. Admission was by ticket, costing six pence each. Each ticket bore a numbered coupon which entitled the holder to participate in the drawing of £500 worth of prizes. Tickets promising a variety of prizes, including a grand piano, £85 worth of furniture down to five shillings, were also sold in the city and sales reached an amazing 115,000. Some individuals bought blocks of 30, 40 and 50 and one gentleman a block of

120. When the lists had been closed all the tickets were fixed to a huge revolving target, 16 feet in diameter. Then a hand-picked group of prominent citizens took it in turns to shoot arrows into the revolving target to determine prize winners until all 150 prizes were claimed. The event was a great success and with all the prizes being donated Manningham made a profit of £1,700.

The cash raised cleared most of the club's debt but did little to save Northern Union football at Valley

Parade. Manningham soon began a series of meetings with two gentlemen actively involved with Association Football. The meetings soon intensified, and it became common knowledge in Bradford that Manningham were holding talks with supporters of 'socker' (the name given to Association Football). The club held their AGM in May 1903. The meeting was a stormy affair lasting two hours with the first hour an ill-tempered attempt to create order. Eventually the chairman Mr Alfred Ayrton gained enough control of the gathering to paint a depressing picture of the financial situation of the club and spoke of the constant struggle to keep Northern Union football in Manningham. He was backed by local businessman Tony Fattorini, who was later to be involved in the Bradford Northern Union club switching to Association Football. Both speakers repeatedly told the meeting that Northern Union football simply did not pay and then Mr Ayrton finally revealed the club's ambitions and proposed the Manningham Northern Union Club disband and form an Association Football club. The resolution was passed, and the name Manningham Football Club soon disappeared to be replaced by Bradford City AFC.

With photography still developing, newspapers would often employ local artists to attend games and produce sketches which highlighted significant incidents during matches. This sketch of the Yorkshire v Lancashire County Championship match played at Headingley on the 14 November 1903 was produced by Amos Ramsbottom and published on the front page of the Manchester based *Athletic News*.

The game was played with 12 players on each side with six forwards.

The Yorkshire followers voiced several reservations regarding the line-up of the teams. Their main concerns were that the reductions in the forwards would restrict the main advantage that Yorkshire teams held with their strong forwards. Historically, county sides from the broad acres had strong agile forwards, skilful in scrummaging and loose play, and Lancashire had skilful backs with great pace. The first half of the game was described as 'bright, open and interesting.' Yorkshire's forwards had the best of the play, but the advantages gained were squandered by poor finishing by the backs. The opening points were scored by Lancashire when the Broughton Rangers pair Bob Wilson and Andy Hogg combined perfectly to carve open a gap for Hogg to score a try. Salford's James Lomas converted with an outstanding kick. Scotsman Hogg later scored an unconverted try in the corner.

The game ended with 8-0 victory to Lancashire and the 12-a-side experiment had been a great success with some delightful open football witnessed by a crowd of 11,000. Lancashire adapted well to the 12-a-side

LANCASHIRE LOSE AT HALIFAX.

On the line

Hilton dodged and kicked well

Farrar outmanoeuvred Hogg and Gifford, and scored the first try for Yorkshire.

Tyson's first try

Taylor played a safe game at back.

Leytham was unlucky in hitting the post.

competition and won all their four games and the Championship. Their backs were a strong combination of skill, strength and superb pace. In the 16-5 defeat of Cheshire at Wheater's Field, Broughton, the three-quarters Jack Fish, Bob Wilson and Andy Hogg each scored a brace of tries and Fish added two goals. On 9 December the trio hit top form during the 42-0 trouncing of Durham and Northumberland at Horsley Park, South Shields. Warrington's Jack Fish scored three tries and kicked four goals. Bob Wilson crossed for a brace of tries and Andy Hogg scored a solitary try. Salford half back James Lomas also scored two tries and two goals.

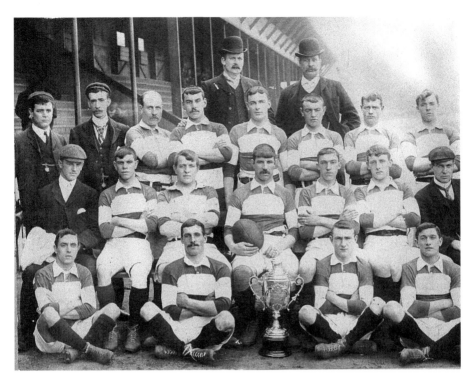

The Hull FC 'A' team with the Northern Union Yorkshire County Junior Challenge Cup at the Boulevard in 1904. The final, contested by Hull A and Castleford-based Whitwood Colliery, was held at Kingston Rovers' Craven Street ground on Easter Monday. A good crowd of 4,452 witnessed the game with gate receipts of £82. The Hull men started well and soon launched a series of attacks on the colliers' line. The Whitwood defence was strong and resisted the constant pressure well. However, Hull eventually created a breach in the colliers' defence. Oliver gained possession from a scrum and sprinted over the line for a try which D'Arcy failed to convert. Immediately afterwards Whitwood created a chance but Portsmouth was soon caught and bowled over. At half-time Hull were leading 3-0. The second half started with sustained pressure from Whitwood, and Burton soon crossed for an unconverted try. Hull retaliated well, and Oliver missed an easy chance. The Hull men continued to pressurise the colliers' defence and Salt soon crossed for a try which D'Arcy once again failed to convert. The game ended without a goal being kicked and a 6-0 victory to the Hull A team. The cup and medals were presented by Mr F. Lister, the Yorkshire president. Oliver, Salt and D'Arcy went on to make limited first-team appearances for Hull FC.

Haworth Northern Union club with the Keighley Charity Cup in 1904. Haworth defeated Keighley Olicana 3-0 in the final. It was the last time the cup was contested under Northern Union rules. A public outcry erupted in the town about the final, which was said to have been contested in 'near war-like conditions' and the whole competition and final was conducted in an unsportsmanlike attitude with far too much general rough play. The following season the cup was contested under Association Football rules and control.

The Cheshire County side that opposed Lancashire in October 1904. Cheshire had started the season in great form with a 5-2 defeat of Cumberland at Prenton Park, Birkenhead. The famous victory was witnessed by a crowd of only 1,000, which was a sad reflection on the perilous state of Northern Union football in the Cheshire outpost. Birkenhead Wanderers

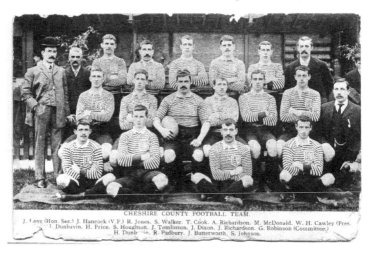

CHESHIRE COUNTY FOOTBALL TEAM.
J. Love (Hon. Sec.) J. Hancock (V.P.) R. Jones. S. Walker. T. Cook. A. Richardson. M. McDonald. W. H. Cawley (Pres.
I. Dunbavin. H. Price. S. Houghton. J. Tomlinson. J. Dixon. J. Richardson. G. Robinson (Committee.)
H. Dunb in. R. Padbury. J. Butterworth. S. Johnson.

Northern Union club had played their home fixtures at Prenton Park in a ground-sharing agreement with Tranmere Rovers AFC. Birkenhead had made the decision to leave their St Anne's enclosure in the summer of 1903. The arrangement failed and, unable to fund a fixture at Barrow, they decided to leave the Northern Union on 11 October 1904, just two days before the Cheshire County fixture. The game against Lancashire was played at Irwell Lane, Runcorn, and attracted a crowd of 3,000, probably boosted by the fact that the Cheshire team contained eight Runcorn players. Cheshire started well and, following sustained pressure on the visitors' line Joe Richardson, the Runcorn half back scrambled over for an unconverted try. It was to be the only score of the game. However, the second half was keenly contested with Cheshire competing well. Cheshire's famous win was their first victory over Lancashire since 1898.

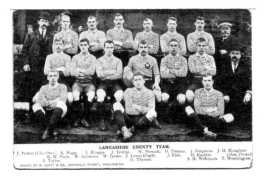

The Lancashire County side that opposed Cheshire in October 1904.

The cover of a souvenir programme produced for Archie Rigg's benefit game in 1904. The benefit was a great success, with 10,000 witnessing Halifax's 13-3 victory over Huddersfield. James Archie Rigg was an immensely talented half back and a very popular player. Rigg joined Halifax RFU in 1891, making his debut in the 'A' team game against Rochdale Hornets 'A'. He stayed with the club when it decided to join the Northern Union in 1895 and made the transition, scoring 67 points in the first season. In 1896/97 Archie Rigg topped the points-scoring chart with 112. Rigg soon caught the attention of the Yorkshire county selectors

and made a total of 32 appearances for the white rose representative team. For Halifax he played in 333 games.

Hull Kingston Rovers and Halifax in action in 1905.

The image appears to show Kingston Rovers moving the ball to their backs following the break-up of a scrum. The ground is Craven Street, off Holderness Road, east Hull. The club moved to Craven Street in 1894/95 when they left the Hull athletic ground, off the Boulevard in West Hull, after their three-year lease ran out. Craven Street was the former home of the old Southcoates club and had two basic stands and wooden-plank terracing.

A different image of action from the Hull Kingston Rovers v Halifax game. This view appears to capture Kingston Rovers players dribbling the ball during a forward rush. A lone Halifax player is preparing to stop the onslaught bearing down on him. Such forward tactics were a surviving relic from the Rugby Union game.

ROVERS v HALIFAX.

A fixture list for the Broughton Rangers club 1905/06 season. A rare piece of Edwardian ephemera. The Manchester-based club ended the season in third position of the First Division. The club excelled in the Challenge Cup, reaching the semi-final. However, the Rangers were defeated by the resurgent Hull Kingston Rovers 10-6, a game witnessed by 12,659 at Belle Vue, Wakefield.

BROUGHTON RANGERS
Fixtures for 1905-6.

Sept.16.	Warrington	away
" 23.	Swinton	home
" 30.	Barrow	away
Oct. 7.	Rochdale Hornets	home
" 14.	Oldham	away
" 21.	Wakefield Trinity	home
Nov.11.	Wigan	away
" 18.	Widnes	home
" 25.	Hull	away
Dec. 2.	Rochdale Hornets	away
" 9.	Bradford	away
" 16.	Leigh	home
" 23.	Barrow	home
" 25.	Salford	home
" 26.	Halifax	away
" 30.	Warrington	home
Jan. 1.	Runcorn	away
" 6.	Wakefield Trinity	away
" 13.	Salford	away
" 20.	Oldham	home
" 27.	Hunslet	home
Feb. 3.	Hull	home
" 10.	Swinton	home
" 17.	Leeds	home
" 24.	Widnes	away
Mar.10.	Hunslet	away
" 24.	Leeds	away
" 31.	Dewsbury	home
Apr. 7.	Dewsbury	away
" 13.	Swinton	away
" 14.	Bradford	home
" 16.	Halifax	home
" 21.	Runcorn	home

The Cumberland County side which opposed Lancashire at Central
Park, Wigan, on 7 October 1905. The Northern Union had changed the
restrictions regarding team selection for county teams. Players were now
able to represent their county of birth and not the county in which they
played their club football. The new ruling allowed Billy little, Bill Eagers
and Joe Ferguson to play in the Cumberland XV. However, Jim Leytham
and James Lomas elected to stay with the Lancastrians. The Cumbrians
started well and worried and bustled the home side. Their constant
pressure soon gave them the lead when, following a sustained battering
of the Lancashire defence, the Wath Brow half back Jenkinson got the
ball and bounded through a gap and over the line for a fine unconverted
try. Following a series of blunders and wild passes between Wilson and
Leytham, Lomas secured possession, charged for the line and transferred
to Jack Fish, who scored in the corner. In the act of grounding the ball, Fish
was bundled into touch and collided with the railings, breaking his collar
bone. A doctor attended Fish and immediately decided he should leave the
field of play. Lancashire brought Rees of Salford out of the forwards to plug
the gap. During all this drama Little failed with the conversion attempt.

With the teams locked at 3-3 the second half was played in a continuous
downpour of heavy saturating rain which had a great effect on the game.
The *Athletic News* correspondent wrote, 'the second-half play was about
as poor and uninteresting as it is possible to imagine.' In the final minute
Little made a clever but unsuccessful drop at goal. Its failure confirmed
the draw.

With Cheshire leaving the competition due to difficulties finding players, the county games were contested by Cumberland, Lancashire and Yorkshire. Cumberland and Lancashire ended joint first with three points each. To create a champion county a play-off game at Central Park resulted in another 3-3 stalemate and the honours were shared.

In 1905 the Northern Union introduced the Lancashire and Yorkshire Challenge Cup competitions. Worried about the advances of Association Football, the Union were confident that the new knock-out competitions would revive interest in the handling code of football.

HUNSLET WIN THE YORKSHIRE SENIOR CUP.

This superb illustration captures the inaugural Yorkshire Cup Final contested by Halifax and Hunslet. A preliminary round was contested with junior clubs, Outwood Church, Featherstone Rovers and Leeds-based Saville Green taking part. Saville Green defeated Brighouse Rangers 10-0 to create a Leeds derby game against Hunslet in the first round, which the Parksiders won 14-0.

The final was held at Park Avenue, Bradford, and rewarded the Northern Union's confidence in the venture when 18,500 witnessed a well-contested and exciting match. Halifax started the game well with their forwards more dashing and determined than the Hunslet pack. The Halifax men gained most of the possession from the scrums and this led to the first try when classic play from half backs Riley and Hilton created the opening for Williams to transfer to Drummond who crossed for an unconverted try in the corner. The try led Hunslet's captain Albert Goldthorpe to grab control of the game and to orchestrate his team's tactics. The experienced Goldthorpe knew the strength and ability of Hunslet's forwards and with a series of short kicks to touch he transferred play to within striking distance of the Halifax line. Albert's brother Walter soon kicked a penalty goal. Albert employed the same tactics and from a scrum under the Halifax posts he dropped a neat goal. The continued forward assaults on the Halifax line gave Albert the opportunity to drop two more goals, Walter another penalty and wingman Charlie Ward a try. Albert's goals were all scored when he gathered the ball from the rear of a scrum and sent the ball between the posts before the Halifax defenders could get close to him. The illustration captures perfectly one of the times Albert collected the ball from the scrum. Towards the end of the game the Halifax team were a completely beaten side, unable to compete with the outstanding fitness and stamina of the Hunslet XV, who won the game 13-3.

John 'Jackie' Mason was one of many footballers from the north west who 'went south' to join leading Yorkshire and Lancashire Northern Union clubs. Mason hailed from Morecambe and first played for the Morecambe Parish Church club as a centre. His competence soon attracted the attention of the premier club of the seaside town, and after a short time in the reserve 15 he was drafted into the senior side of the Morecambe Football Club. Mason's partner in the three-quarters was Bob Wilson, who would later join Broughton Rangers and become one of the finest footballers in the early

Local Football Celebrities.

JOHN MASON.

years of the Northern Union. Mason remained loyal to Morecambe when the club joined the Northern Union, but his performance in a play-off match against Widnes in 1900 soon alerted Wigan. The Wigan committee quickly approached Morecambe and signed Mason for the 1901/02 season. 'Jackie' Mason's diminutive figure (he was 5ft 5in tall and weighed 10 stones and 5 pounds) hardly seemed suitable for Northern Union football. However, it was said that 'Mason will stand like a rock if the whole of the front rank is rushing down upon him' and his solid play at full back earned for him the title 'Safety Pin'. One of great, long-forgotten nicknames of the early days of Northern Union football, Mason was granted a benefit game by Wigan and on 6 April 1910 Wigan defeated a 'Rest of the league team' 27-11 at Central Park. Playing in the 'Rest' side were prominent players such as Anderson, Turtill, Gunn, Padbury and Winskill.

Fred Goodfellow of Dewsbury in 1906. Fred Goodfellow was born in Sharlston, Wakefield, and played his early football with Sharlston RFU and then the Sharlston junior Northern Union club. He joined Wakefield Trinity in 1898, playing all his games in the 'A' team, and was then transferred to Holbeck in 1899. When the south Leeds-based club resigned from the league, he was transferred to Hull FC, making his debut on 3 September 1904. Goodfellow made 54 appearances for Hull, scoring eight tries and 66 goals, including 11 goals from 12 attempts when Hull trounced Leigh Shamrocks 52-0 in the first round of the 1905 Challenge Cup. Fred was on the move again in 1906 when he was transferred to Dewsbury and made his last move when he re-joined Sharlston in 1910. In 1921 a severe injury forced Fred to retire from football at the age of 41.

A collage of caricatures featuring Alf Carmichael which appeared in the *Hull Daily Mail* in 1907.

Alf 'Bunker' Carmichael was one of the great full backs of the Edwardian era of Northern Union football. He made his debut for Hull Kingston Rovers at Batley on 18 April 1903. Bunker played his football in the Rovers second team until he became the regular first-team full back in 1906/07. He was a strong, solid defender and exceptionally gifted goal-kicker. During the 1907/08 season he kicked 81 goals and then in 1908/09 he kicked 78 goals. He topped the goalscoring chart for four consecutive seasons from 1909/10 to 1912/13 with 127 in 1910/11. In October 1910 Carmichael kicked a record 14 goals in Rovers' 70-13 thrashing of Merthyr Tydfil.

Unfortunately, ill health interrupted his career and he made his last appearance for Rovers against Wakefield Trinity in late January 1919. At the time of his retirement Alf Carmichael had made 338 appearances, scored 12 tries and kicked 723 goals, a total of 1,482 points. Bunker became the landlord of the Queen's Hotel in Charlotte Street, Hull. However, his health deteriorated and he died in September 1921.

A cartoon commenting on the complex new league Championship scheme which had been adopted for the 1905/06 season. The Northern Union had introduced several new league structures since 1895/96, the majority failing because the union's committee was dominated by the big clubs interested in fixtures that would bring in the most money. They had little regard for the struggling junior clubs who had flocked to join the new code to improve their standing. From 1902/03 to 1904/05 a two-division system seemed to be working well. Then following a radical proposal by the

Yorkshire County committee and a series of meetings involving all clubs the Northern Union formed a new system which would create a single league of 31 clubs who would be free to arrange their own fixtures but had to play every team from their own county and fulfil a minimum of 20 games. The competition would then be decided on a percentage basis. Leigh were the first champions with 48 points from 30 games and a percentage of 80. However, alarm bells rang when it was found that Oldham had played 40 games to gain 58 points and fourth position with 72.5%.

The Ebbw Vale Northern Union club which contested the newly formed club's inaugural fixture at Keighley on 7 September 1907. The players for that historic and courageous venture into NU football are: Back row: T. Lewis, A. Rodway, J. Hitchens, J. Brain, W. Sanders, J. Lawrence, W. M. Evans. Middle row: Gordon Jones, Tom Davies, A. Monks, 'Chick' Jenkins, J. A. Evans. Front row: Councillor J. Cameron, Lewis, Arthur Price.

A decent crowd estimated at 4,000 gathered at Keighley's Lawkholme Lane ground expecting to witness a good exhibition of football from the visitors. However, they had little chance of victory. They were far from ready to be thrust into a strange new game against a tough, experienced professional team. A large crowd had given the Welsh team a hearty send-off from the Great Western Railway station at 10.10pm on Friday evening. The journey through the night took 12 hours, not the best preparation for such an important fixture. From the kick-off the result was only ever to be a Keighley victory and they were 26-3 victors. The Yorkshire spectators gave the Welshmen a superb reception and when the ball sped across the line from a scrum to enable Evans to score a try the crowd erupted in 'hearty cheering'.

A cartoon published in the *Hull Daily Mail* captures Charles Brain in action during his debut for Hull Kingston Rovers on 19 October 1907. Rovers signed Brain, the 6ft, 13.5 stone, 20-year-old from Harrogate Rugby Union Club when club officials had witnessed the dashing three-quarter score a hat-trick of tries against the Hull and East Riding Rugby Union Club. The young Brain had played football for his regiment in Ireland prior to joining Harrogate. Arriving in Hull on Thursday, 17 October, Brain was immediately selected for the first-team game against Bramley on Saturday 19

FOOTBALL CARTOON.—No. 244.

V·PER

BRAIN, THE ROVERS' NEW " SIX-FOOT " WING, MAKES FOR THE LINE.

October. Although unfamiliar with the Northern Union style of play he created a favourable impression, especially when he made a terrific dash to score his first try for the Rovers, helping them to a 29-5 victory. Later in the game he made a similar assault for the line which prompted one committee man to comment, 'If he keeps at that nothing less than a locomotive from the railway will stop him.' His robust displays soon earned him the nickname 'Slasher'.

When war broke out Charles Brain volunteered for active service and in 1914 he embarked to France and was captured at the Battle of Mons on 24 October of that year. He spent the next four years in captivity and was finally repatriated in 1918. Although his war-time experiences had taken their toll, 'Slasher' made his final appearance for the Rovers on 5 March 1919.

Charles 'Slasher' Brain made 180 appearances, scoring 74 tries and three goals.

Halifax at Fartown 20 April 1907.

The Halifax Northern Union club was a major force in the Edwardian era and at the end of the 1906/07 season the club were top of Northern Rugby League table with 56 points from 34 games (82 per cent). The infamous 'percentage' scheme was still in place but with a new method of deciding the champions. A top-four play-off was introduced where the first-placed club would play the fourth and second play third, with the victors contesting a final. Halifax defeated Keighley 9-4 and across the Pennines Oldham beat Runcorn 11-3 to set up the final at Fartown, Huddersfield. The Northern Union followers in both counties were captivated by the new system and a crowd of 13,200 gathered to witness the game. Halifax continued the outstanding form they had played throughout the winter and their brilliant football overwhelmed Oldham 18-3. The Halifax forwards were superior, with Bartle and Bulmer each scoring tries. However, the *Athletic News* praised Billy Little, who Halifax had signed from the Cumberland-based Seaton club in 1901, recording, 'Little played a great game, his fielding, kicking and tackling being of the best.' Salford-based referee F. Priestley had a severe attack of cramp five minutes from the end of the game and was replaced by J.C. Lumley of Leeds. The incident had little effect on the game.

The players are – back row: Midgley, W.W. Williams, Wedgwood, T.S. Dodd (president), Bulmer, Rickets. Robinson, Bartle, Brearley, Foster, Morris. Middle row: Swinbank, Atkins, Littlewood, Joe Riley, Longhorn, W.J. Williams, Ward, H. Morley. Front row: Grey, Hilton, Eccles. Far left on the front row, Tommy Grey, who would later join Huddersfield, is nursing 'Smut' the cat. The little black cat had wandered into the club's pavilion at the end of November 1907 heralding a run of 17 unbeaten games. He was soon adopted as the club mascot and became a firm favourite of the players and a celebrity in Halifax.

The Halifax team had an enthusiastic reception when they returned home with the trophy. The steam engine which hauled the team from Huddersfield was decorated with the blue and white colours of the club. Two brass bands were waiting at Halifax to escort the players and officials

to their headquarters for a celebratory dinner. Among the telegrams received was one from the officials and players of Oldham congratulating Halifax on their splendid victory.

Smut the cat, the Halifax mascot.

A cartoon highlighting the crisis at Bradford, published in the *Bradford Daily Telegraph*.

In May 1907 the foundations of the Northern Union were seriously damaged when founder members Bradford decided to leave the union to form an Association Football club. The Bradford club had reported a loss of £600 the previous season and had formed the opinion that Northern Union football would not pay. A series of special committee meetings were held and several solutions to the financial problems were discussed. The most ludicrous plan was that the club resign from the Northern Union and revert to the Rugby Union game. In hindsight the very notion that the RFU would welcome back a club that had been a leading member of an organisation that had all but decimated the Rugby Union code of football in Yorkshire was absurd. The Bradford club released the idea of fixtures with

Rugby Union clubs in the south of England and the border region of Scotland that would pay was simply pure fantasy. Eventually, despite denying the idea on several occasions, the club announced they would be competing in the Association Football southern league for the 1907/08 season.

A Hull Kingston Rovers team from the 1905/06 season, with the side comprising 15 players. It was the last season of 15-a-side as in the following season the Northern Union made the momentous decision to shed two forwards and create 13-a-side teams. At the same time the Northern Union also created the 'play-the-ball' rule to bring the ball back into play following a tackle. It was a Renaissance for the Northern Rugby Football Union. The union had eventually realised that to make their code of football more attractive to spectators the game needed to be transformed on the field of play, far more than ever-changing league structures. It was one of the most revolutionary concepts since the original split in 1895. The Northern Union had now created its own unique identity. In 1895 the bold pioneers had broken away from the control of the southern gentry and now with its own exclusive structure it had become a new and different game to RFU and soccer. These innovations shaped the code into an exciting, fast-moving and skilful game where the ball was almost constantly in play.

HULL KINGSTON ROVERS F.C. 1905-6
T.JACKSON C.SEYMOUR D.MULLINEUX A.WINDLE W.T.OSBORNE J.CATH G.JOHNSON (SEC) W.BROWN
W.BENT H.SHERWOOD D.REES A.STARKS (CAPT) H.SINCLAIR W.PHIPPS C.J.HAMBRECHT
H.SHANN (TRAINER) J.GORDON (VICE CAPT) G.H.WEST J.BARRY W.JOWETT

Second from the right on the front row is George Henry 'Tich' West, who had signed for the Rovers in 1901. Hull Kingston Rovers drew the Cumberland-based junior side Brookland Rovers in the first round of the Challenge Cup and the tie was scheduled to be played up in Cumberland. Anxious to avoid a loss-making journey to Ellenborough, the home of

Brookland, the Kingston Rovers officials offered Brookland £80 and a share of the gate to transfer the fixture to East Hull. The Cumbrians agreed and were completely outclassed by an in-form senior side who overwhelmed them with a score of 73-5. 'Tich' West had a superb game, scoring 11 tries and kicking ten goals for a record total of 53 points. Eye witness accounts described some of West's tries as 'brilliant and some as generous gifts from his teammates.' When West retired in October 1908 he had scored 98 tries and 65 goals for Hull Kingston Rovers.

An illustration from the *Athletic News* depicting Ebbw Vale's first game in Lancashire on the 21 September 1907. The team had left their home town in the early morning for the long train journey to Oldham, not the best preparation for a game against one of the best Lancashire sides. Newspaper reports recorded that the Welsh team's 'forwards played well with some splendid kicking and tackling, although, their tackling was too rough at times.' The players' passing ability was described as 'erratic and poorly executed'. Oldham were never troubled and were 26-5 victors.

This advert from 1906 shows Herbert Hadwen, who was another Northern Union footballer who became landlord of a pub. Hadwen had initially played his football with Morecambe before moving south to join Salford and he then crossed the Pennines to become a member of the Halifax club in 1902.

Hadwen enjoyed great success with Halifax and made 29 appearances, scoring six tries and five goals during the 1902/03 Championship-winning season. He kicked two goals to help Halifax win the Challenge Cup Final in 1903 and one goal in the following season's final when the Yorkshire club were once again cup winners. On his retirement he remained in Halifax and became landlord of the town centre Corporation Inn.

Alex Laidlaw of Bradford also became the landlord of a pub. He is pictured outside the Prospect in Bradford.

The Widnes team that opposed Barry in a home game on 24 October 1908. The Welsh club was handicapped from the very start of their adventure in the Northern Union due to their location and, like Ebbw Vale and Merthyr Tydfil, soon realised that early morning starts and long railway journeys to the north of England were not the best preparation to oppose the experienced professional sides against which they played. The *Athletic News* commented: 'The Welshmen are a team of promise; they are big enough, have a fair turn of speed and their courage could

not be questioned. They are not afraid of passing the ball about but some of their handling was listless and inaccurate. What they lack is method and this fault can be overcome with experience.' However, they came up against a team with method and experience and Widnes had little difficulty in gaining possession of the ball. Hicks was superb at half back and the three-quarter line was sound and effective. Widnes ran in seven tries and ended the game 31-6 victors. Barry never really adapted to their new code of football. The club was badly funded and received very little help from the Northern Union, apart from a £5 grant to help with travel expenses to away games. In their one and only season Barry finished 29th out of 31 clubs. The Widnes players are – back row: George Highfield (trainer), Joe Carr, Sam Aspey, Bill Rigby, Herbert Lloyd, Peter McCarthy, George Aspey, Fred Smith (secretary), unknown. Middle row: Jack Lambert, Harry Curtis, Bob Jones, Johnny Moran, Ernie Ince, Harry Taylor. Front row: Jack Lally, Fred Hicks.

The Broughton Rangers side that defeated Swinton 8-0 on 14 September 1907. The Rangers were the Lancashire Cup holders and on the previous season's league form were favourites to defeat Swinton. Broughton had one of the finest three-quarter line-ups in the Northern Union, with Scot Andy Hogg and North Lancastrian Bob Wilson the architects of the bewildering and dazzling combined movements that were a major feature of the club's method of play. However, Swinton had devised a strategy to combat Rangers' style, and despite being considered man-for-man no comparison to

BROUGHTON RANGERS.

Broughton in physique their determined plan of close marking and prompt and hard tackling prevented the Rangers' combination from developing any serious movements. The Lions of Swinton's tactics were simple but effective and their performance was enthusiastically celebrated in the press reports of the northern newspapers. The new 13-a-side and play-the-ball rules introduced in the previous season were beginning to create new thinking and innovative styles of play and indeed a new code of football.

A St Helens team from the 1907/08 season. The club had never really been successful in Northern Union football up until this point. The 1907/08

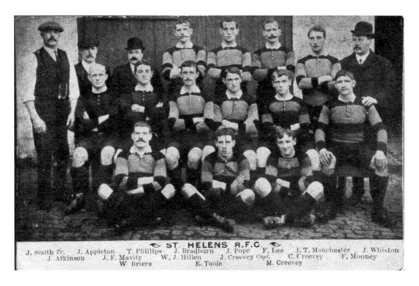

season was the 13th of Northern Union football and it was the poorest for the Saints, who finished in 25th position out of 27 clubs and bottom of the Lancashire League. They were knocked out of the Lancashire Cup 17-14 by Oldham in the first round and were beaten 21-10 by the New Zealand tourists.

A Bradford Northern team line-up at their new Greenfield Athletic Ground in 1907/08.

The Northern Union enthusiasts connected with the Bradford club were quick to create a new club following the debacle at Park Avenue in 1907, when the Bradford club left the Union to take up Association Football. The new club, Bradford Northern Union football club, later to be known as Bradford Northern, was formed in late May 1907 and soon secured a lease on the Greenfield Stadium, Dudley Hill, from the owners William Whitaker's Brewery. A crowd of around 6,000 attended the match, which the new Lord Mayor of the city, John Arthur Godwin, kicked off. Bradford's forwards were the most effective but a weakness at half back enabled Huddersfield to gain an 8-5 victory.

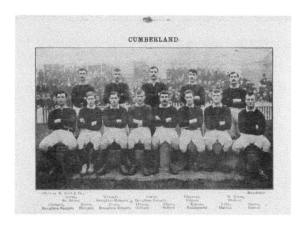

The Cumberland County team that defeated Lancashire at Wheater's Field, Broughton, on 5 October 1907. Cumberland won 7-3 with a try from Kitchen and goals from Little and Lomas and they went on to defeat Yorkshire 7-3 at Whitehaven and were crowned County Champions.

The Lancashire county side which opposed Cumberland County on 5 October 1907.

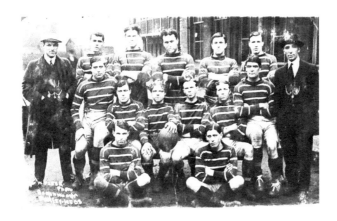

A Leeds A team around 1907. Second teams were rarely photographed and there are no records of the players

Hunslet with the Yorkshire Cup in December 1907. Back row: W.H. Cockerham (secretary), Smales, Farrar, Higson, W. Hannah (trainer), Wilson, W. Wray, Cappleman, J. Lewthwaite (chairman). Middle row:

Eagers, Randall, W. Ward, A. Goldthorpe, Jukes, Brookes, W. Goldthorpe. Front row: C. Ward, Place, Smith, Batten, Walsh. Hunslet were well into their ground-breaking 'All Four Cups' season and their style of football was a revelation in Northern Union football.

    A good crowd of 15,000 witnessed the Parksiders overwhelmingly defeat a weakened Halifax side 17-0 at Headingley. However, the Parksiders' methods won them little praise outside their own supporters. The Hunslet forwards dominated the game, winning five of every six scrums. The *Leeds Mercury* reported: 'In pushing power, in clever footwork, they were far ahead of those opposing them. Again and again they carried the ball with them.'

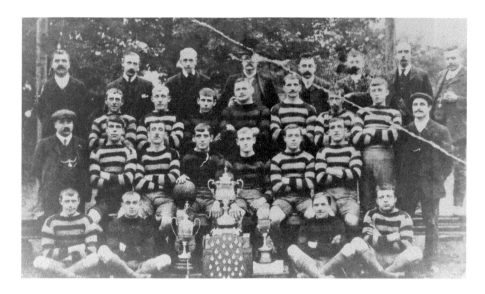

The Beverley side in the 1908/09 season. The juniors had a superb season and are pictured with the East Riding League Cup, Hull and District Challenge Cup and the WFB Eyre Cup. On 27 February 1909 Beverley defeated professional club Ebbw Vale in the first round of the Challenge Cup.

The line-up is – back row: T. Gilson, T.E. Charlton, J. Brooks, W.F.B. Eyre (East Riding League president), F. Hoggard, C. Greenside, J.R. Brooks and H. Verity. Third row: G.H. Holgate, T. Long, M.U. Holgate, R. Windle, J.T. Brown, G.W. Billton, A. Grice, F. Boyes (hon treasurer). Second row: E.H. Butt (hon sec). Front row: A. Verity, J.W. Johnson, W.G. Richardson, T. Skinner.

A Huddersfield team at their Fartown base, 1908/09. Back row: Gronow, A. Wilson, J. Binns, W. Ainley, W. Brook, A. Hirst, F. Charlesworth, A. Swinden, H. Bennett (assistant trainer). Front row: A. Bennett (trainer), J. Davies, J. Jagger, H. Wagstaff, W. Kitchen, D. Holroyd, J. Bartholomew, E. Wrigley.

The Wigan team that played Hunslet at Central Park on 12 September 1908. Wigan won 18-10 with tries by Todd, Johnston, Leytham and Ramsdale and three goals by Thomas

The players are, back row (left to right): Silcock, Cheetham, Ramsdale, Blears, Johnston, Whittaker, Brooks, Prescott. Front row: Gleave, Miller, Todd, Leytham, Sharrock, Thomas, Jenkins.

The Hunslet team that opposed Batley on 19 September 1908 at Parkside. Second from the right on the back row is Walter Goldthorpe, the youngest of the five Goldthorpe brothers who played for Hunslet. It was Walter's first appearance for Hunslet in the 1908/09 season as he had been in dispute with the club's committee when they asked him to play away from his normal

Photo by R. Scott & Co.   **HUNSLET F.C.**   *Manchester*

W. Hoyle.   W. J. Eagers.   H. Place.   W. Hannah (*Trainer*).   F. Smith.   W. Goldthorpe.   W. Batten.
   T. Walsh.   H. Wilson.   J. W. Higson.   A. E. Goldthorpe.   W. Jukes.   J. Smales.   W. Wray.

position. Walter felt that at his age he should be allowed to continue as normal as a centre. He had refused to play in earlier games, much to the irritation of the committee. Eventually Walter's attitude led to him being granted a free transfer and cross-city rivals Leeds soon signed him in November 1908. Walter had made 389 appearances, kicked 116 goals and scored 67 tries for a total of 443 points under Northern Union rules for Hunslet. He made a great contribution to Leeds's successful Challenge Cup campaign in 1910, scoring tries in the draw with Hull in the final and in the victory in the replay. Walter decided to retire, aged 37 at the end of that season. He had made 51 appearances, scoring 16 tries and kicking 44 goals for Leeds.

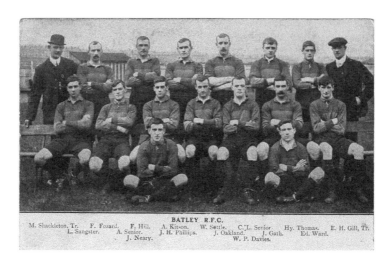

M. Shackleton, Tr.   F. Fozard.   F. Hill.   A. Kitson.   W. Settle.   C. L. Senior.   Hy. Thomas.   E. H. Gill, Tr.
L. Sangster.   A. Senior.   J. H. Phillips.   J. Oakland.   J. Gath.   Ed. Ward.
J. Neary.   W. P. Davies.

BATLEY R.F.C.

The Batley side that opposed Hunslet on 19 September 1908.

A rare surviving postcard advertising a joint benefit match in 1909. Harry Wilson and Tommy Walsh were two of Hunslet's famous forwards and had been members of the celebrated Hunslet pack that had been termed 'the terrible six' during their renowned 1907/08 season, when the south Leeds club were the first team to win 'All Four Cups.' Tom Walsh, a policeman, had made his debut for Hunslet in 1896/97. Harry Wilson made his debut for Hunslet in the 1898/1899 season. Wilson had previously played Rugby Union for Morley, Methley, Castleford, Rothwell and Yorkshire. During

'PARKSIDE'. HUNSLET.

🖝 DON'T FORGET 🖝
THE
HARRY WILSON & TOMMY WALSH
JOINT BENEFIT.
HUNSLET
VERSUS
HULL KINGSTON ROVERS.
DECEMBER 18th, 1909.

NO OTHER FIRST CLASS MATCH IN LEEDS ON THAT DATE.

his Northern Union career Wilson represented Yorkshire and opposed the inaugural New Zealand tourists in all three test matches. The benefit game was a disappointment to Walsh and Wilson as fine weather on the morning had transformed into rain by the time of the kick-off, reducing the crowd dramatically. However, the Hunslet committee decided to donate part of the gate to the benefit fund.

An illustration from the front page of the *Athletic News,* November 1909, depicting action from the Wigan v Leigh Lancashire Cup Final. A crowd of 14,000 at Wheater's Field, Broughton, witnessed Wigan beat Leigh 22-5. The game was described as 'men and methods'. Wigan had embraced the new, faster style of play, with its emphasis on the play-the-ball creating more expansive play for the three-quarters. Wigan's methods were described thus: 'their ideas were good, rapid handling, correct passing, and support to the man with the ball.' Leigh's system of play was the opposite and old fashioned: 'the ball was held too long, and the runner invariably preferred to punt instead of pass. Combination and finish were missing.' The *Athletic News* commented: 'matches are not won with defensive play alone and punting pure and simple invariably provides opportunities for your opponents.' Northern Union football was moving forward to a game those early innovators could have never envisaged.

Huddersfield 1909/10. The ambitious Fartown-based club were constantly in the process of building a squad of players to create teams to bring success to the club.

Huddersfield defeated Batley 21-0 in the Yorkshire Challenge Cup Final at Headingley in November 1909 to collect their first-ever trophy under Northern Union rules. Batley were unlucky that afternoon when they lost Thomas, Ward and Oakland to injuries. Oakland did return but, down to 11 men,

Batley were overwhelmed by the pace and movement of the Huddersfield backs, with all four of the three-quarter line scoring tries. The Fartown side's tactics were simple strong, fast and straight running and constant backing up of the man with the ball.

The Yorkshire County side that defeated Lancashire 27-14 at the Boulevard, Hull, in early November 1909. The white rose team's 27 points created a record for County Championship games. It was Yorkshire's first victory in the season's Championship. They had travelled to Maryport in early October but the game against Cumberland was abandoned ten minutes into the second half because of the extreme rain, wind, and a partially flooded pitch. The two county committees were unable to agree to a venue for a reply and the Northern Union decided the Championship would be shared

YORKSHIRE Northern Rugby Union.

DEVEREUX   F. BOYLAN   HALEY   A. S. CROSSLAND   HILL   W. D. LYON, Esq.
   Hull   Bradford   Bradford   Wakefield   Batley   Touch Judge.
J. B. COOKE, Esq.   J. DAVIS   H. PLACE   H. WILSON   JARMAN   F. W. OLIVER   J. W. WOOD, Esq.
   President,   Huddersfield   Hunslet   Fartown   Leeds   York   Secretary.
         P. ECCLES, Halifax.   F. SMITH, Hunslet.   W. DAVIS, Batley.

by Yorkshire and Cumberland, who had both beaten Lancashire to be joint leaders with two points each.

The Swinton team that opposed Warrington at Chorley Road on 9 October 1909. Warrington defeated Swinton 15-0 thanks to solid forward play and

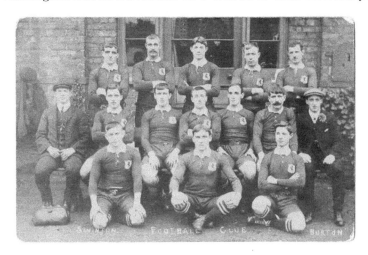

a moment of classic wing play from Warrington's Jack Fish. The Swinton Lions started well, their forwards gaining good possession from the scrums and launching a series of rushes into the Warrington defence. The clever Warrington backs soon struck and slick passing led to a marvellous dash down the wing by Jack Fish which ended with Jenkins crossing for a try under the goal posts. Thomas converted, later in the first half Fish scored again with another typical dash and the visitors led 10-0 at half time. In the final minutes of the game Bradshaw crossed for a converted try and Warrington had earned a 15-0 victory.

Alf Mann was a strong, robust forward who played with Bradford around 1905/06. Mann became Bradford Northern's first test player when he played for the Northern Union in the first and third tests against the Australians in the 1908/09 series. In 1909 the player was involved in a controversy when he turned up at Hull Kingston Rovers with Mr T. Bayliss, the Bradford Northern secretary and fellow player T. Surman. Bayliss collected £120 in notes and gold for the players' transfer fees and gave £25 to Surman and £20 to Mann. Hull Kingston reported the transaction to the NU and Bayliss was relieved of his office and immediately vanished. The Northern Union ordered Mann and Surman to pay back the money they had received to Hull Kingston. Both players were retained on the Bradford

club's register. In 1909 Mann was suspended by Bradford Northern for failing to turn up for a game with Hunslet and using abusive language to committee members, and he was immediately placed on the transfer list, later being officially transferred to Hull Kingston Rovers. Mann became a crowd favourite at Craven Street and made 224 appearances, kicking four goals. With his strong, dashing play, he also scored 50 tries. Mann captained the side during the war-time emergency leagues and played his last game for Rovers in a Yorkshire Challenge Cup third-round home defeat by Huddersfield. Following this game Mann moved back to the West Riding to re-join Bradford Northern.

A Leeds team from the 1908/09 season. Leeds had signed Joseph Aloysius Lavery, who had been a member of the 1907/08 New Zealand tourists. The full back/centre/half back was the first overseas player to be signed by the club and had previously played for Temuka, Christchurch Albion, Canterbury and the South Island. Lavery impressed the committee when he played in a pre-season trial at Headingley in late August 1908 and was immediately drafted into the first team for the game against Broughton Rangers at Wheater's Field on 5 September. Broughton defeated Leeds 17-13 despite losing their captain Bob Wilson with a broken collar bone. Lavery played well and one eye witness account recorded that, 'the New Zealander contributed sound defensive play and was quick to spot an opportunity'. Joe Lavery played ten games for Leeds, scoring four tries, and he later played for Leigh and Salford before returning to New Zealand in 1913 where he played for Linwood in the Canterbury Rugby League competition. He was wounded in the World War One and returned to Linwood. The Leeds line-up for the photograph taken at Broughton is as follows:

Back row (left to right): Morn (trainer), R. Ward, J.W. Birch, J.A. Lavery, H. Ibbotson, S. Williams, J. Harland (assistant trainer).

Middle row: Webster, F. Young, Thomas (captain), S. Whittaker, E. Ware, Harrison.

Front row: Desborough and R. Jones.

Chapter 3

THE BIRTH OF INTERNATIONAL TOURS – KIWIS, KANGAROOS AND LIONS 1907 TO 1911

Albert Henry Baskiville. 'Bert' was a forward with the Oriental Rugby Union Club in Wellington, New Zealand. The young Baskiville was a promising player and a great student of the handling code. He read about the exploits of the new 'Northern Union' game in England and set a series of events in motion that were to spread the 13-a-side code to Australia and New Zealand. Baskiville wrote to the Northern Union proposing a tour of England and Wales by New Zealand footballers eager to play Northern Union football. The Union welcomed the idea and

soon contacted him to initiate the complex arrangements for the tour. In Wellington Baskiville, a great organiser, began to secretly contact players he thought would be interested. The New Zealand RFU heard of the venture and promptly banned Bert from attending games in New Zealand, declaring the tour to be 'professional'.

Lancelot Beaumont 'Lance' Todd was a clever half back from Auckland. He joined the tour squad in 1907 and soon became a member of the management committee, helping in organising the tour. He excelled playing Northern Union football and played in all the test matches. He joined Wigan in 1908 and then moved to Dewsbury in 1914. In 1928 Todd took the position of team manager at Salford and he also commentated on Rugby League matches for BBC Radio. Todd

was a member of the Home Guard during the war. On 14 November 1942 Lance Todd died in a traffic accident when he was returning home from Home Guard duties in Oldham.

His name is immortalised in Rugby League with the annual Challenge Cup Final man-of-the-match award the Lance Todd Trophy.

A cartoon depicting 'the phantom team' arriving in England.

THE NEW ZEALAND "PHANTOM"

To protect the players who had signed up for the tour, Baskiville and his fellow selectors refused to disclose the names of anyone involved. The NZRFU instantly labelled the squad a 'phantom team,' reporting that the public were being deceived by Baskiville and his supporters and that the tour would not take place. The New Zealand Agent General in London denounced the tour in an interview published in the *Morning Post* asking the names of the players and even the name of the ship on which they were to sail. The following day Mr Joe Platt, the Northern Union secretary, introduced truth to the debate when he replied: 'I announced over a week ago that the team have sailed on the SS *Ortona*.' Prior to sailing, tour member George Smith had contacted a friend in Sydney who organised three games for the tour party. Baskiville's men had by now been dubbed 'the All Golds,' a reference to their so-called professionalism. The 'All Golds' were victorious in all three games they played against NSW. The matches were played under Rugby Union rules and all three attracted huge crowds. The party then stopped at Ceylon where they defeated a Ceylon Rugby Union side 33-6 at Havelock Racecourse, Colombo. Reports of the game wired to England and published in the *Hull Daily Mail* recorded that the All Blacks were 'simply marvellous and with their terrific pace they spread across the field like a stream of human arrows.'

Herbert Henry 'Dally' Messenger.
Dally Messenger was one of the finest rugby players in Australia. He opposed the All Blacks in the games in Sydney and was invited to join the tour by the selection committee. Dally had recently joined the newly formed NSWRL and therefore severed his connection to Rugby Union.

He must have believed that a chance to play Northern Union football in England would develop his career in Rugby League when he returned to Sydney. Messenger's decision was a massive boost to the tour, Australian Rugby League, the Northern Union and international football. Messenger was a big name in the handling code and his tremendous displays on the football field would add hundreds to a gate wherever he played.

The tourists on their arrival at the Midland Railway Station, Leeds.

The tourists had landed in Folkestone and then transferred by train to London when, following a brief stay, they travelled to Leeds, arriving in the early evening to a tumultuous welcome. The Northern Union committee and several prominent players were waiting to greet the party. An estimated crowd of 6,000 people, who crowded the platforms, burst into tremendous cheering as soon as the players appeared. The cheering continued until the party boarded the Hunslet club's char-a-banc, which was decorated with the chocolate-and-white colours of the South Leeds club. 'Bumper' Wright, the NZ captain, then called for three cheers for the people of Leeds, which were followed by the stirring Maori war cry and further cheering. The crush of people was so dense that Boar Lane and Briggate were closed to traffic and the trams. The team eventually made their way to their headquarters, the Grand Central Hotel, where a vast crowd had gathered. Inside the hotel the New Zealanders were entertained with a lavish dinner by the Northern Union.

The full squad gathered at Headingley, Leeds.

The All Blacks practice at Headingley.

The tour party committee of Baskiville, Smith, Johnston and Todd soon realised they had to get their players fit following the long journey to England. The Northern Union and the Leeds club allowed the tourists full use of the Headingley ground and facilities. The tourists played a series of practice games to improve fitness and acclimatize themselves to the new game they were about to play. Mr J. H. Smith the experienced referee and administrator carefully observed these practice sessions and explained the rules and finer points of the Northern Union game to the players and commented in an article in the *Athletic News*, 'one thing is certain the All Blacks are infinitely superior as regards carefully thought out methods.' He went on to say, 'these men who have come so many thousand miles to demonstrate their capacity ask questions which compel the conclusion that a great part of the time occupied in travel has been spent trying to master the intricacies of our game.'

The All Blacks stride on to the field at Barley Mow, Bramley.
Wednesday, 9 October 1907 – at last the highly anticipated opening game of the first-ever tour by an overseas team had arrived. The tourists began their tour with a fine 25-6 victory witnessed by a crowd of 6,000. The All Blacks struggled with the new game in the first half, especially in the forwards. Bramley played well and Sedgwick was a constant worry to the visitors. In the second half the tourists settled down and produced some good football, with Dally Messenger delighting the crowd with a great try and an excellent display of goal-kicking.

A scarce action image from the Bramley v New Zealand game. Several newspaper accounts of the match compared the tourists to the Rugby Union players of 1905. A somewhat pointless comparison, with the

various rule changes initiated since that tour which had transformed Northern Union football into a different game to the Rugby Union football witnessed two years earlier.

The All Blacks tour was very popular and Albert Baskiville was soon recommending the famous 'Zam Buk' in newspapers across the north of England.

A newspaper illustration depicting action from the tourists' game against Huddersfield on 12 October 1907. The fixture had been eagerly awaited in the week prior to the game and a crowd of 9,000 gathered at Fartown to witness the match. The All Blacks had made seven changes to the side that played at Bramley. From the kick-off it became apparent that Huddersfield's methods were to stop the tourists gaining control of the ball. The home forwards played well, gaining possession from the scrums five times out of six. At half-time the home side had a lead of 8-3. In the second half the tourists became a different team; their forwards gained more possession and the three-quarters played with far more confidence. The diminutive Lance Todd, making his debut, had a spectacular game, his pace causing the home side no end of problems. In the final ten minutes Huddersfield simply collapsed completely and the tourists scored 16 points, giving them a 19-8 victory. The *Hull Daily Mail,* a great supporter of the Northern Union, and the tour commented that, 'instead of falling off towards the finish in every department the New Zealanders were going stronger than ever, which indicates how well trained the players are, the All Blacks never say die; they struggle until the last second.'

A rare surviving score card from the tourists' match against Wakefield Trinity on Wednesday 23 October 1907.

The All Blacks made several changes which had an adverse effect on their performance. Wright, Cross and Johnston were missing from the forwards, and Todd and Wrigley absent from the backs. Trinity were at full strength and their strong forwards dominated the game. The New Zealanders were a completely different side. Jim Gleeson at half back had a poor game and his almost constant kicking was a major tactical blunder which achieved little. Practically the whole of the tourists' 13 players kicked far too often. The home team's Cumberland-born James 'Jimmy' Metcalfe was one of the finest and safest full backs in the Northern Union. The experienced veteran

Metcalfe fielded every kick that flew into his domain with confidence and many of his returns launched the Trinitarians on devastating excursions into the visitors' defences. Wakefield held a 5-2 lead and looked like winners until deep into the second half, when Rowe crossed for an unconverted try to add three points to the two scored by Messenger in the first half and create a 5-5 stalemate. Albert Baskiville later commented on the game: 'We badly underestimated our opponents.' The *Leeds Mercury* correspondent commented on the tourists' tactics: 'There were no more severe critics of the fatuous policy of the New Zealanders than their colleagues who watched the game from the touchline.'

The Leeds and New Zealand teams pose together before the game at Headingley on 26 October 1907. The tourists picked their strongest side for the match, anxious not to repeat the poor display seen at Wakefield. The forwards were said to be strong in loose play but once again their poor scrummaging let them down. The *Leeds Mercury* commented that, 'The tourists' forwards lose their effectiveness by waiting to form a scrum on their own orthodox lines. In consequence their opponents secure the first push, which invariably gives them the ball.' Once again the backs made full use of the little possession they had and their play was described as 'positively startling' and at times 'their handling of the ball bewildering'. The All Blacks were very popular in Leeds and a good crowd of 12,321 witnessed their 8-2 victory.

NEW ZEALAND v. LEEDS
(NORTHERN UNION)
October 26th, 1907.

The cover of the programme for the fixture with Leigh on Wednesday 20 November 1907. 8,000 witnessed Leigh defeat the tourists 15-9. The first half was even, Messenger kicked two superb goals. and Webster, following an 'irresistible dribble by the Leigh forwards', scored a try which Molyneux converted. With the wind and the slope in their favour, the home forwards were on top form and simply swept the All Blacks six aside, *the Yorkshire Post* commenting, 'They swamped the New Zealanders in the scrummages, beat them in the open by their impetuous rushes and expert dribbling.' The New Zealanders were never allowed to settle, such was the control Leigh had of the ball and their attempts to create passing movements

were soon stopped by Leigh's deadly tackling. They tried high kicks and following up, but Clarkson at full back caught every kick. The home side were now pressing for a famous victory and began to change their tactics, alternating passing and cross-kicking with brilliant forward bursts. Leigh winger Neville added two tries, Molyneux dropped a goal and for the All Blacks Cross scored a try which Messenger converted. It was the tourists' third defeat. They had previously lost to Wigan and Barrow.

A newspaper illustration depicting the Oldham v All Blacks game at the Watersheddings, 23 November 1907. Oldham were one of the strongest sides in the Northern Union and were top of the league table and must have expected an easy contest against a touring side still struggling to secure possession from the scrums. However, the All Blacks were a different team, and although their forwards did not gain as much of the ball from the scrums as Oldham in loose play 'the fiery footwork of Wright, Cross

and Johnston was more than equal to that of the home side'. The first half was a tight, exciting 40 minutes and at half-time Oldham had a 5-2 lead. The second half opened with a fierce snowstorm, weather conditions the majority of the All Blacks had never played in or even seen. They soon mastered the conditions and once again the forwards were constantly dangerous with their fierce, determined running and footwork breaking into the Oldham half. For once it was the tourists' backs that were disappointing. *The Yorkshire Post* recording that, 'as a body they appeared to suffer from a lack of confidence.' Then, with only ten minutes remaining, a marvellous piece of play by George Smith finally carved out an opening in the Oldham defence. The *Athletic News* correspondent described the action: 'By skilful control of the ball, Smith dribbled right from his own '25' to the home line, where Lavery, with a fine burst of speed, dashed up and beat Thomas for possession, putting the finishing touch to a grand movement by registering a try.' Dally Messenger converted, and the visitors were only one point in arrears. The All Blacks continued to push but the magnificent Oldham defence stood firm and the game ended with an 8-7 victory to the home side.

The cover of the official programme for the Runcorn match on Wednesday 27 November 1907.

Heavy rain on the morning and early afternoon of the game had reduced the attendance to 5,000 and made the Canal Street pitch heavy going. It was one of the All Blacks' worst displays of the tour. The forwards were beaten for possession and without the ball the backs did little but defend. The 'Linnets' of Runcorn were superb, their forwards gaining control of both the scrums and loose play. Within minutes of the kick-off Runcorn were pressing the tourists' line and with the ball won from a scrum,

Official Programme
GRAND FOOTBALL MATCH
RUNCORN
v.
NEW ZEALAND
Wednesday, Nov. 27, 1907.
PRICE   ONE PENNY

'Jolley, Watton, Butterworth and Deakin engaged in passing, which ended in Deakin scoring a fine try in the corner'. Jim Jolley missed the conversion attempt. James 'Jim' Jolley had a great game at half back, his constant probing and service to his three-quarters creating the openings for all three of Runcorn's tries. Early in the second half Jolley set in motion a movement that involved the whole of the Linnets three-quarters and resulted in a try for Moran. Towards the end of the game, with the visitors a totally beaten side, smart passing between Jolley and Butterworth gave Deakin the time and space to score his second try and give the home side a famous 9-0 victory.

The cover for the programme issued by Bradford Northern for the game against New Zealand on 10 December 1907. It is a remarkable testament to the popularity of the All Blacks tour that so many of these ephemeral items have survived for over 100 years. A large crowd gathered in the city centre to greet the tourists. However, heavy rain soon began to saturate Northern's Greenfield Stadium high above the city at Dudley Hill. The Bradford Northern committee were expecting a crowd of 25,000 but the ceaseless rainfall reduced this to a mere sprinkling of 2,000. Amongst the spectators braving the weather were the curious members of the Bradford City Association Football Club. There was a lot of disappointment

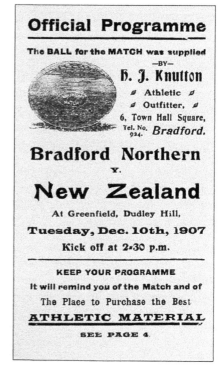

at the absence of Bradford's George Marsden, the team captain and firm favourite of the Greenfield crowd, and the All Blacks preferring Wright and Messenger to act as gatemen instead of playing. There was a 'feeble cheer' when Gomer Gunn led the home side on to the pitch. Within minutes the saturated Greenfield pitch was churned into a muddy quagmire with several pools of water. Somehow the players carried on in the face of near gale force winds lashing the rain across the pitch. Actual descriptions of the play are scarce with most newspapers concentrating on the atrocious weather conditions. *The Bradford Daily Telegraph* correspondent recorded that, 'it was a glorious exhibition in the circumstances that prevailed, and Bradford are to be congratulated on their play. Surman, Brear and Gunn were the heroes of the home side, and on the visitors, there were none to compare with Lavery.' It was a famous 7-2 victory for Bradford Northern and a great boost for Northern Union Football in the city following the debacles at Manningham and Bradford FC.

The Yorkshire side that opposed the All Blacks at Belle Vue, Wakefield on 18 December 1907. Despite a very pleasant afternoon, a poor crowd of only 3,000 gathered to witness the game.

Both teams were at full strength for the tourists' 20th game and their first against county opposition. The opening minutes of the game were strange when, following the first two scrums, the New Zealand captain 'Bumper' Wright left his position in the forwards to act as an extra half back. Even with a man less the tourists beat Yorkshire in pushing, gaining possession and rushing. Messenger was soon prominent and dropped a superb goal from a pass by Wynyard. Surman equalised with a penalty. Then a quick pass from Lance Todd allowed Wynyard to dash through some weak tackling to score a try, which Messenger converted. A poor pass from Phil Thomas to Farrar allowed George Smith to swoop in to gather the ball and race down the field and then kick the ball over the head of Taylor. A frantic race between Smith, Farrar and Lile ended when second row forward Lile

Yorkshire v. New Zealand

WAKEFIELD DEC. 18, 1907

dropped on the ball for a brilliant try. Messenger converted and soon after Surman kicked a penalty for the home side.

Early in the second half George Smith had to leave the field with a chest injury, later diagnosed as a broken rib. Even without Smith the tourists were still in control and Messenger, with a clever dodging run, set up a tremendous movement when the ball was flashed across the line for almost three-quarters of the length of pitch. The Yorkshire defence scrambled in time to prevent a try but minutes later Messenger kicked a towering penalty goal from the centre. The 'Tykes' were now hopelessly beaten, and another fine movement ended with a try for Rowe, which Messenger converted with his seventh goal of the match. It was a magnificent 23-4 victory to the tourists. The Belfast based *Northern Whig,* in a well-observed and detailed account of the match, commented: 'In loose play the New Zealanders were complete masters, and at times made the Yorkshire defence look very elementary.'

Herbert Henry 'Dally' Messenger, pictured here early in the tour, was a remarkable success against Yorkshire, kicking seven goals. During the tour he made 29 appearances, scored seven tries, kicked 60, often spectacular, goals and scored 141 points.

Caricatures of the goal-kicking styles of Hunslet's Albert Goldthorpe and All Black Dally Messenger captured during the Hunslet v New Zealand tour game at Parkside on 26 December 1907.

Hunslet were the Yorkshire Cup holders and were enjoying great success in the league. They had a tremendous pack of forwards who were known as the 'Terrible Six'. Behind this powerful forward combination, the 'Parksiders' had a sturdy set of backs including a young and hugely powerful Billy Batten. Hunslet also had their

immensely popular captain Albert Goldthorpe, who at 36 years of age was still a master tactician and gifted goal-kicker.

A huge crowd of 20,000 gathered at the South Leeds ground to witness the highly anticipated match against the tourists. The spectators were not disappointed, the game was an intense struggle brimming with incident. The All Blacks were missing George Smith, who was nursing a broken rib, and Hunslet were missing Fred Farrar and were almost without Albert Goldthorpe who had only decided to play at the last minute. The All Blacks started well and at half-time were leading 9-0 thanks to a try and a goal from Wrigley and two long-range goals from Messenger. Hunslet gradually clawed their way back into the game when Albert Goldthorpe kicked three goals. With a quarter of an hour remaining Dally Messenger launched a towering kick from three yards inside his own half and against a strong wind that sailed straight between the posts. The game seemed to be beyond the Parksiders until the final minutes when Wilson, from what looked like an offside position, dropped on a loose ball for a try. The drama continued up to the last kick of the game when, with the scores locked at 11 all, Albert Goldthorpe's conversion kick to win the game drifted sideways and struck the upright and rebounded harmlessly back onto the field. The game was a robust one, the *Leeds Mercury* commenting: 'There were times when the players exceeded legitimate keenness and Smith, the Hunslet half back, was sent off the field for kicking Wright when he was on the ground. There were also some cases of fists up, while a Hunslet player flung the ball at an opponent's head on being tackled.' At the close of play Edgar Wrigley asked Albert Goldthorpe for his shirt, and, as generous as ever, Albert disrobed on the field and Wrigley waved the white jersey aloft in triumph.

The England team that played the All Blacks at Central Park, Wigan, on 11 January 1908. A crowd of 10,000 endured a bitter cold afternoon and were rewarded with a fast-entertaining spectacle. England were lucky to gain an 18-16 victory, with the tourists throwing away two or three easy chances to score. The home side started the game well, their forwards strong rushing building a good platform for the backs. Eccles, the Halifax winger, scored the first try with a clever dodging run past Messenger. Later, the dashing Runcorn forward Padbury, taking a clever short pass from Ferguson, swept over the line for a try which Ferguson converted to give England an 11-5 half-time advantage.

Once again, the New Zealanders' forwards were poor, the *Athletic News* commenting: 'There was much of a muchness about the forwards, whose indifference to dribbling was their greatest failing.' The tourists' backs

England v. New Zealand.

AT WIGAN. JAN. 11, 1908.

excelled in the second half, the *Athletic News* commenting: 'Their passing was splendid as were some of the short services and return passes.' The *Bradford Daily Telegraph* correspondent was also impressed by the high-speed moves of the tourists, describing the first try: 'Wrigley launched a long inside pass to Rowe who immediately transferred to George Smith who dashed forward then passed to Todd. The latter was hemmed in by Taylor and Leytham and thereupon he passed the ball over their heads to Wynyard, who outpaced his opponents and scored a brilliant try.'

Hubert Sydney 'Jum' Turtill, the New Zealand full back was quite a portly young man at the beginning of the tour, which led the players to nickname him 'Jumbo' which was shortened to 'Jum' when he shed his excess weight. His performance against England prompted the *Yorkshire Post* to record: 'Turtill gave a splendid exhibition at full back, he has really no superior in the Northern Union, his tackling, fielding and kicking being of the best.' Turtill made 33 appearances, scoring one try and five goals. He later joined St Helens and was killed in action in World War One.

A newspaper illustration depicting the ill-fated first Northern Union v New Zealand test match at Headingley on 25 January 1908.

The test was heavily criticised by the northern newspapers, the majority of which had been loyal supporters of the tour. Most thought that the game should have been played much earlier in the tour when the tourists were still fresh and their play attracting good crowds. The *Yorkshire Post* recorded some very critical comments: 'The New Zealand footballers are fast losing whatever reputation they made for themselves in their matches before Christmas. They are doing badly and the public interest in their doings is on the wane.' The tourists had performed well in a new game played against the best of teams, masters of the 13-a-side code and often in adverse weather conditions. However, the long tour and the harsh physical and mental demands were beginning to affect the players. The game itself was a poor one, a sad exhibition of a tired, jaded team against a strong experienced Northern Union side that had almost full control and ruthlessly exploited the flaws in the tourists' methods. The All Blacks' forwards were described as being, 'slow, heavy and stale and some of them were out of condition'.

Their attempts to form a competitive scrum had no coordination and, as the game advanced, they seemed to pack in one line and this only had the effect of enabling the home forwards to rush easily through them.

At the end of play the Northern Union were 14-6 victors, witnessed by a crowd of 8,000.

The York and New Zealand players pictured before the game at Clarence Street on 29 January 1908. York were a mediocre side and were not expected

to challenge the tourists. However, the Minstermen raised their game and defeated the All Blacks 5-3, witnessed by a crowd of 5,000. The tourists' forwards played a fine game and a strong rush by their pack set up the first try when Wrigley, Kelly, Wynyard and Tyne combined to allow Rowe to cross in the corner. Later, York broke away and Oliver passed to Hughes who launched a huge cross kick, which Kelly fumbled, allowing Garbutt to follow up and score near the posts. Plimmer converted and York had a 5-3 lead.

The scorecard from the York fixture.

A group of action images from the second Northern Union v New Zealand test match played at Stamford Bridge, Chelsea, on Saturday, 8 February 1908.

The decision to play the test in London was a courageous initiative by the Northern Union and the first determined attempt to spread the code of football away from its solid northern origins. Most newspapers welcomed the endeavour with excellent coverage of the game. However, The *Yorkshire Post,* which had been a constant critic of the Northern Union since its inception, devoted more column inches to the previous Rugby Union All Blacks tour than the actual match at Chelsea and went so far as to comment that the attendance was as good as could be expected in view of the international 'proper' at Richmond. The *Daily Telegraph* commented that many of the 14,000 spectators were puzzled by the rules but were enthralled by 'the tremendous pace which all the men maintained, the accuracy of the passing and safe fielding of the ball, and the wonderful length of the kicking.' The form of the tourists was in total contrast to that, which they had shown during December and January. They were fitter and 'all round gave a grand display'. The All Blacks' forwards were the main architects of the convincing 18-6 victory, their superb scrummaging a revelation and an inspiration to their teammates. The *Athletic News* commented on the ineffective display of the Northern Union: 'They were out of touch with their surroundings and never settled down to their proper game. They allowed the Colonials to set the pace and were seemingly content to take second position.' The Northern Union was beaten for possession for two-thirds of the game and the half backs were often smothered by Wrigley. George Smith was a shining light, ever alert to the unorthodox, and his try came after a wonderful passage of play. From a successful scrum stand-off Wynyard gave a swift pass to George Smith who sprinted down the field. The *Athletic News* described the movement: 'Smith drew the defence in the direction of Messenger, outwitting Llewellyn and Eccles who crowded about Messenger, then Smith swerved towards the centre, and rounding Taylor, raced away for the line, which he crossed with ease.' The All Blacks' other points were scored by a try from Lance Todd, a brace from 'Massa' Johnston and three goals from Dally Messenger. Leytham and Eccles scored tries for the Northern Union. With the test series tied, everything hinged on the third test.

The Northern Union and New Zealand players at the Athletic Ground, Cheltenham, prior to the third test match on 15 February 1908. Albert Baskiville's meticulous planning made sure the tourists were fully prepared for the deciding test and they arrived in Cheltenham on Thursday, making their headquarters at the Fleece Hotel. The Northern Union's preparations

were incompetent. Most of the committee arrived on Friday evening, but the players travelled on early Saturday morning, most rising at 6.30am, with one player actually leaving home at 3am. They then had to endure a five-hour journey and, arriving in Cheltenham an hour and a half before the kick-off, the players had to take part in a formal luncheon. Heavy rain fell for most of the game, making the ball greasy and hard to handle, but the pitch was in superb condition and, although muddy in places, held firm. The owner of the enclosure, Mr Bailey, had put a great deal of effort into making sure the occasion was a success. He had erected a temporary stand. It was thought that the attendance of 4,000 would have been far greater but for the severe weather. The Northern Union started the game well and 18-year-old debutant Billy Batten was a powerful addition to the team. The tourists matched the Unionists for most of the first half, but the backs struggled in the conditions. Minutes before half-time, scrum half Jolley seized the ball from a scrum and burst over for a try, which White converted. On the restart the All Blacks adopted their tactics to suit the conditions, with both forwards and backs dribbling the ball forwards. The Northern Union players were now rapidly tiring and struggling to hold the tourists. Messenger and Todd scored tries to give the visitors the lead. In

the final 20 minutes the New Zealanders' determination to win the game created a great deal of rough play and New Zealand forward Cross, who had been warned four times, was sent off for punching. The private battles continued, with Oldham-based referee Bill McCutcheon doing a great job in controlling the fighting. Then with barely two minutes remaining the immensely strong forward 'Massa' Johnston hurled himself over the line for a try that gave the tourists a hard-fought victory and the first test series. The game was not the classic open game the Northern Union had wanted to help spread 13-a-side football to the south. However, the crowd who braved the weather seemed to enjoy the skills and passion of the players involved.

The cover for the tourists' final game of the tour at St Helens on 22 February 1908.

The 39th game of the tour was badly affected by the weather. Rain had fallen throughout the morning and had developed into a gale, driving heavy

rain straight down from post to post at Knowsley Road. The players braved the conditions and George Smith kicked off into the face of the gale. With the wind behind them, the Saints' players pounced on the ball and at once dribbled to the tourists' line, where from a scrum the home side gained possession and quickly transferred the ball to Manchester, who crossed for a try which Matt Creevey failed to convert. A further try from Lee and two James Creevey goals gave the home team a 10-0 advantage at half-time. In the second half, with the wind in their favour, the visitors did practically as they liked and tries were scored by Tyler, Wynyard (2) and Tyne. Messenger kicked three goals. In his first game of the tour Albert Baskiville also crossed for a try to make the result a 21-10 victory to the

New Zealanders. It was a strange game to end the tour as the weather conditions had contributed greatly to the tourists' success. However, throughout the tour the harsh northern weather had at times interrupted the tourists' style of football, so perhaps it was ironic that the weather had helped them for once.

The menu cover for a dinner held by the NSWRFL to celebrate the departure of the 1908 Kangaroos.

The first 'Kangaroos,' the Australian Rugby League tour party, in 1908. The 35-strong party had an incredible, gruelling 45-match schedule.

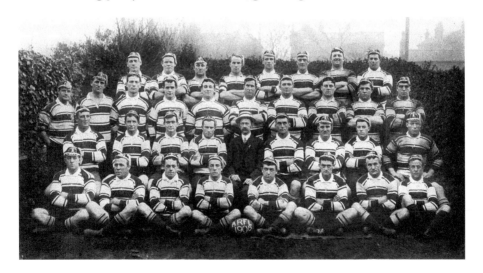

A rare surviving booklet produced for the Kangaroos tour.

A newspaper illustration of the Australian visit to Rochdale on Saturday, 10 October 1908. Trade was poor and money scarce in Rochdale and with the price of admission for tour games doubled from six pence to a shilling, the attendance was a meagre 3,000. The game was poor, with the tourists criticised extensively by northern newspapers. The *Athletic News* commented: 'The Kangaroos, as a team and as individual players, were disappointing in the extreme, the ball was thrown about in haphazard fashion and combination was a missing quality. Of real effort there was none.' Despite these failings the tourists opened the scoring when 'Messenger secured the ball in the home "25" and after a dash for the line passed to Morten, who hurled himself over the line with two men clinging to him.' Messenger converted. In the closing minutes the Hornets pressed the visitors' line with some determined play. The game became a little too rough and the referee had to reprimand several players. The tourists' defence held firm and the game ended with a 5-0 victory to the Kangaroos.

The York and Australian tourists pose before the tour game on Wednesday, 14 October. The Kangaroos were still struggling with Northern Union rules and tactics and had made changes for the match against York. The *Yorkshire Post*, never a supporter of the Northern Union and always quick to criticise, commented: 'A touring combination of this kind is supposed to contain reserve forces of sufficient excellence to lift the team above the level of an ordinary club side, this has not been done.' York started the game well and after 15 minutes play Danielle made ground down the wing and launched a superb cross-kick to enable Raywood to cross for an unconverted try. The tourists soon took the lead when Rosenfeld collected the ball from a scrum and dashed over the line for a try, which Messenger converted. The Australians held on to their two-point lead until about two minutes from time when, with a defeat for the home side looking almost certain, 'Oliver picked up a loose ball and coolly dropped it over the bar' to give York a well-deserved draw.

The Kangaroos perform their war cry before the game against Salford at The Willows on Saturday, 17 October 1908. Following their poor displays in their earlier fixtures, the tourists played well, although they were still not fully acquainted with the rules and tactics of Northern Union football. They seemed to be adopting Rugby Union methods with far too much kicking and little attempt to open the game out with passing movements. The *Athletic News* commented: 'Their tackling was sound, their punting good and their catching of the ball safe. The backs were speedy, and their defence was above reproach. Passing runs, however, they did not attempt in the style of our leading clubs. The transfers were too slow, and the men took the ball practically standing still.' Play in the first-half hardly flowed and several penalties resulted from obstruction. Messenger kicked two goals for the tourists and Mesley landed a

goal from a mark and Preston added a second from a clever drop. The teams changed ends with the game balanced at 4-4. In the second half both teams were searching for a victory. Salford took the lead when, from a mark, Mesley kicked a goal. The tourists were spurred into action and Morton 'made a glorious run, swerving by man after man, and then passed to Devereaux who beat one or two opponents before he got over.' Messenger missed the conversion by inches. Minutes later Lutge kicked a goal to give the visitors a slender three-point lead. The Kangaroos made a major tactical blunder when they removed Walsh from the forwards to the three-quarters and dropped Messenger back to assist Bolewski at full back. The bizarre changes weakened the tourists' ability to gain possession from the scrums and the Salford six took full advantage of the situation, winning enough control of the ball to keep the Kangaroos pinned in their own half. The visitors defended well but eventually after a constant Salford onslaught John burst through and passed to Willie Thomas who crossed in the corner. The conversion attempt failed, and the game ended 9-9. The 6,100 spectators had witnessed a fast and exciting exhibition of Northern Union football.

The Leigh team that defeated the Kangaroos 14-11 at Mather Lane on Wednesday, 28 October.

The match created tremendous interest in Leigh, and it was reported that the roads leading to the ground were thronged with people well before the 3.30pm kick-off. 6,000 spectators packed into the ground with hundreds of unemployed men watching for free from the railway embankment that overlooked the ground. Also attending were the complete Australian squad, several prominent NU officials and many leading journalists. The scene was set for an historic event and on the field of play the match lived up to its expectations. The game started with strong attacking play from

both teams and within five minutes a passing movement by the Kangaroos ended with Frawley crossing for a try in the corner. Messenger failed with the conversion attempt. Minutes later Messenger made a grave error when playing the ball, kicking it hard into the open. The loose ball was caught by Sam Johnson who immediately sprinted over the line for a try, which Clarkson failed to convert. The tourists responded well when their backs combined with the forwards in a great movement which took them to within yards of the line. The Leigh defence hesitated when they thought an Australian had been properly tackled and waited for him to play the ball when he passed to Abercrombie, who rushed over line. The try was allowed, and Messenger kicked the conversion. Leigh replied when Billy Smith collected a loose ball, drew the defence and passed to Herbert Bennett, who fooled the defence and gave the ball to Bob Neville, who scored in the corner. The game continued at a thrilling pace and from a clever interception the tourists once again swept forward and their short accurate passing created an opening for the big forward O'Malley to charge over for a try. The Leigh players still sensed a victory and soon Bennett charged down a kick by Deane and 'took the ball grandly and running hard gained a splendid try'. Leigh were now almost unstoppable and once again Bennett raced down the right wing, drew the visitors' defence and then launched a kick to the left. Billy Smith took the ball near the line and tipped it over Bolewski, raced over and dropped on it 'amid a hurricane of cheers'. Clarkson kicked the goal and Leigh were leading by three points. In the final 12 minutes the Kangaroos were superb and did everything but score. It was a momentous victory for Leigh and was described as 'one of the finest displays of Northern Union football ever seen.' After the match both teams and reserves, the officials and the Northern Rugby League committee were entertained to high tea at the White Horse Hotel, Leigh, where it was reported, 'Mrs Gee provided a substantial repast.'

Mick Bolewski, who had a great game at full-back for Australia, later joined Leigh and became their first overseas player to make 100 appearances.

A fine sketch of the Kangaroos at Hunslet from the *Yorkshire Evening News*.

Hunslet were one of the strongest and most-feared teams in the Northern Union and the previous season they had won all the four trophies available in NU football. The little south Leeds-based club

had built an outstanding squad of players which was focused around an immensely strong and mobile pack of forwards. Behind the six, tactics were decided by Albert Goldthorpe, a vastly experienced half-back and exceptional goal kicker who with the possession the forwards gained was blessed with the options of launching his forwards in terrifying dribbling rushes or unleashing the pace and handling abilities of the Hunslet three-quarters. Hunslet at their Parkside ground were formidable. Hunslet was a predominantly working-class area with little spare money around, and with the admission fee set at a shilling, a poor crowd of 6,000 attended the game. The tourists set about the game strongly and their forwards were soon rushing towards the Hunslet line, and it was only keen tackling from Eagers and Hoyle that kept them out. A superb heel from a scrum allowed Holloway the time and space to dart over the line for a try, which Messenger converted. Soon after Albert Goldthorpe launched a superb short kick, which Billy Batten followed up and knocked the ball back to Jukes, who scored. Albert failed to convert. Minutes later Deane fielded a clearance by Eagers and sprinted half the length of the field to score a brilliant try, which Messenger converted. Then Hunslet's 'terrible six' set in motion a great rush forward which ended when Billy Batten scored. Albert Goldthorpe kicked his first goal of the afternoon and the teams turned around with the tourists two points to the good. The second half set off at a tremendous pace. Morten extended the tourists' lead when he dropped a goal and later clever passing between Albert Goldthorpe and Billy Batten put Jack Randall over the line for a try, which once again Albert failed to convert. In the final quarter Albert Goldthorpe decided the time had come for the 'terrible six' to test the visitors. He punted the ball high and 'encouraged by the typical Hunslet howl the terrible six bore down upon the waiting Kangaroos.' The *Athletic News* commented on the visitors' brave defending: 'The defence of the colonials was magnificent, and few teams – indeed, I might go further and say no team – could have withstood with success the terrible onslaughts made on their defence in the last quarter of the game. Their courage was unmistakable. The Colonials have the satisfaction of knowing they accomplished a task which to the great majority of Northern Unionists appeared impossible.' The match ended with a well-deserved 12-11 victory to the Kangaroos. It was thought by many that the tourists had still not mastered the crucial, strategic importance of playing the ball and could have increased the margin of the victory if they had held onto the ball more instead of their habit of simply throwing it backwards when tackled.

The Kangaroos endorse 'Zam Buk'.

In 1910, following lengthy negotiations with the Australian Rugby League and a full financial report from a sub-committee, the Northern Union agreed to send a squad to tour Australia and New Zealand. The NU produced a souvenir booklet for the tour.

As soon as the players to tour were confirmed the NU began to kit them out. They decided on Manfield boots at nine shillings and six pence a pair.

Makers of Football . . Boots to the players of

NORTHERN UNION AUSTRALASIAN : TOUR. : : :

Example of boot supplied to order No. 3303. 10/6. : : :

MANFIELD'S FOOTBALL BOOTS
First in public favour and first in sound tested value. This is no mere advertising phrase applied to Manfield's productions, but a well supported and obvious fact, proved by a record of remarkable sales, as well as by overwhelming expert testimony. Over 100 premier clubs of England, Scotland, Ireland, Wales and the Continent regularly wear Manfield's Football Boots

MANCHESTER :—
78, 80, 82 & 84, MARKET St.,
22 & 24, St. MARY'S GATE, ::
55, DEANSGATE, :: :: ::
177, OXFORD ROAD, and at
London and all important towns.

The full squad photographed on their arrival in Australia. The players are wearing the red-and-white hooped jerseys and dark shorts and socks that had been selected for the tour. The red-and-white hoops represented the red and white roses of Lancashire and Yorkshire.

A group of Lions on the high seas en route to Australia.

Fred Smith pictured in his Lions' kit.

Smith was a sturdy half-back who had once been described by Harold Wagstaff as 'one of the strongest and skilful half-backs I ever played against.' Born in Woodlesford near Leeds, Smith had played soccer for Kippax before signing for Hunslet in 1906. He made 12 appearances and scored four tries on the tour.

Wigan's five representatives on the 1910 Tour of Australia. Top left: Bert Jenkins. Top right: Jimmy Leytham. Middle: Johnny Thomas. Bottom left: Jimmy Sharrock. Bottom right: Dick Ramsdale.

A postcard depicting Wigan's 1910 tourists.

The Northern Union team that opposed New South Wales on 4 June 1910. Back row: Jenkins, Winstanley, Ramsdale, Ruddick, Thomas. Middle row: Young, Jukes, Lomas, Boylen, Bartholomew. Front: Webster, Farrar, Smith.

A huge crowd of 33,000 witnessed the Lions lose 14-28 to a strong NSW side. Although both teams were playing under the same NU rules, the tourists were puzzled at referee McMahon's slipshod control of the scrums, especially when it was reported that on many occasions the ball was thrown against the Australians' open side forwards' legs without entering the scrum. There were also instances when the ball went straight through the tunnel and out of the blind side and yet the game carried on. The tour managers were delighted with the size of the crowd and the gate of £1,383. Rugby League was fast becoming the premier handling code in New South Wales.

The cover for the official programme for the first-ever Australia v Northern Union test match held at the Royal Agricultural Showground, Sydney, on 18 June 1910. The tour had created tremendous interest in Sydney, and with Rugby League in the city flourishing a huge crowd of 42,000 witnessed the game.

The team line-ups from the first test programme. The lions were 27-20 victors in a game that was described as 'a perfect exhibition of Northern Union rules.'

The Australian Rugby League had arranged a goal-kicking contest prior to the kick-off. This involved the team captains each attempting five kicks at goal from various positions. Captured here is the action of James Lomas, who landed three successful goals.

Australian captain 'Dally' Messenger attempts a shot at goal during the kicking competition. Much to the dismay of the huge Sydney crowd,

Messenger was only successful with two of his kicks. However, the great 'Dally' did kick four goals during the match.

The star player for the Northern Union was Billy Jukes, the incredibly mobile forward who crossed the line for three superb tries. His third, to complete the first 'hat-trick' of tries by a forward in an Anglo-Australian test match, came when half-back Tommy Newbound passed to Billy Batten, who sprinted to the Australians' '25' and then transferred to the

pursuing Jukes, who galloped over the line. William 'Bill' Jukes was born in Featherstone in 1883. He played his early football with the junior club Featherstone Rovers. In 1905/06 he signed for Hunslet and soon became an influential member of the Hunslet 'terrible six' set of forwards. During the 1907/08 season he played against Oldham in the important Challenge Cup second-round match in the stand-off position when 'he combined admirably with Smith and he had an important share in the scoring of two of Hunslet's tries.'

A group of Lions on their arrival in New Zealand in 1910. There is no surviving record of the names of the players.

The Northern Union footballers are homeward bound from Australia. The financial success of the tour exceeded all expectations.

A newspaper cartoon of the profit the Lions had made. The tour had raised £12,000 and after deduction costs made an outstanding £1,445 profit.

The menu card for a welcome home dinner given in honour of the Lions.

Photo by R. Scott & Co.]   **AUSTRALASIAN F.C., 1911—12**   [*Manchester*

The Australia squad for the 1911/12 tour of England and Wales.

International football was now a major part of the Northern Union. In England the code had settled down and had a firm stronghold in Yorkshire and Lancashire. The 13-a-side code was highly successful in Australia and New Zealand and the squad was chosen from the eight clubs that had formed in 1908 and represented the NSWRL. To help spread the game, four New Zealanders were included to give the squad the title of the Australasian Rugby League tourists. The tour's itinerary was a far more sensible and manageable 35 games rather than the 45 games the 1908 Kangaroos had endured.

A rare surviving souvenir brochure published in Australia prior to the tour. Brochures such as these soon became part of the heritage of Anglo/Australian tours.

S. PEARCE
(Eastern Suburbs).

C. SULLIVAN
(North Sydney).
17

W. FARNSWORTH
(Newtown).

A page from the 1911/12 tour brochure introducing some of the players.

The line-up from the programme for the first game of the tour v Midlands and South players held at the Butts Ground, Coventry, on 23 September 1911. The tourists, who had been training since their arrival in England, looked fit and strong. However, once again the tourists were weak in the scrums. The southern hemisphere players that had visited England before

AT COVENTRY, SATURDAY, SEPTEMBER 23rd, 1911.

AUSTRALIANS v. MIDLAND & SOUTHERN PLAYERS

TO-DAY'S TEAMS.

Season Tickets.	MIDLANDS & SOUTH		AUSTRALIANS.		TO LET!
	1. A. E. WOOD	Back	13. NEIL		
	2. J. COOK	R.W. Back	12. RUSSELL		Advertising Space
GROUND 5.	3. E. WARE	R.C.	11. V. FARNSWORTH		
	4. T. ROBINSON	L.C. Back	10. GILBERT		in this
NEW GRAND STAND	5. J. HOUGHTON	L.W.	9. BROOMHAM		
Wings 7 6	6. T. WHITE	Outside Half	8. W. FARNSWORTH		Programme.
Centre 10 6	7. D. KEYNON	Scrum Half	7. McKIVATT (Capt.)		
	8. A. E. AVERY	Forwards	6. SULLIVAN		
	9. T. WOODS		5. McGEE		
LADIES' TICKETS 5.	10. D. WYBURN		6. FRANCIS		For particulars apply:
	11. W. HUTT		3. SAVORY		
	12. T. HERRIDGE		2. COURTNEY		W. BIRKETT,
May be obtained at the Gate or	13. J. P. OLDHAM		1. CRAIG		36, Grantham Street,
from any of the Directors.	14. L. F. S. BEAVER		14. HALLETT (Reserve)		COVENTRY.
	(Reserve).		15. HALLOWAY		

Referee - - Mr. ROBINSON (Bradford).

PRINTING! ☞

When you want Good Printing done, bring it to us. We are making new customers every week, and, what is more, keeping them.

What is the secret of our success? We can tell you. We do Good Work Promptly, and we do not try to charge more than the job is worth. Give us a trial with your work.

CALDICOTT & FELTHAM, Tel. 260

The City Press, 33, Cross Cheaping.

109

had all struggled with the sheer speed and intricacies of Northern Union scrums and the progression of play following a scrum. The *Midlands Daily Telegraph* correspondent commented: 'Forward the Kangaroos were weak in the scrummages, though had all the half-dozen players borne individually their proper share of the work a different result might have been produced.' The *Athletic News* went further, suggesting that many of the tourists were too big for scrums, commenting: 'They do not get down in the packs. To put it plainly they appear unwilling to bend their backs. Thus, their strength is wasted in that early push which on nine occasions in ten means possession of the ball. Frankly, the Colonial forward apparently desires to shirk the pack and concentrate his energies upon brilliant dashes in the open.' A poor crowd of 3,000 witnessed the match which ended in a 20-11 victory for the visitors. McKivatt (2), Robinson, Sullivan and Viv Farnsworth (2) crossed for tries for the tourists and Russell kicked their solitary goal. Houghton (2) and Wyburn scored tries and Robinson kicked a goal for the home team.

Viv Farnsworth played a superb game for the tourists, his stylish running prompting the *Midlands Daily Telegraph* to comment, 'Vivian Farnsworth ran at times like a deer, flashing past opponents in brilliant fashion and fully justifying all the praise sung about him in Australia.'

The teams published in the Hunslet programme for the tourists' game against Hunslet on 21 October 1911. Once again, the size of the attendance was influenced by the policy of doubling the price of admission to a shilling and

a poor crowd of 4,000 gathered at Parkside, although persistent rain before and during the first-half would also have discouraged many people. Hunslet began the game in splendid form, excelling in the basics of Northern Union football. Their forwards heeled from the scrums, rushed, dribbled and tackled with grit and determination and the backs passed and ran fearlessly and they had, by avoiding foolish kicking, kept the ball in their own hands, and out of those of the speedy tourists. Harry Toft, Hunslet's Welsh stand-off, opened the scoring early in the first half when a clever short pass from Fred Smith outmanoeuvred the tourists' defence. Toft, who revelled in the nickname 'the human corkscrew,' sprinted to right, drawing the tourists' defence, then swerved to left and accelerated to the line and with the cover gaining on him he passed to Bill Jukes who hurtled over the line with two defenders clinging to him. The Parksiders then blundered when they tried to hold the tourists in their own half instead of attacking. It was a big mistake to try to hold on to a three-point lead and McKivat and Francis soon burst away, with McKivat passing to Broomham who scored in the corner. Once again, the conversion was missed, and the game ended 3-3.

Pages from the Hunslet v Australia programme. The Hunslet club published a pen picture of Bill Jukes who had scored a hat-trick of tries against the Australians in the first test match in June 1910.

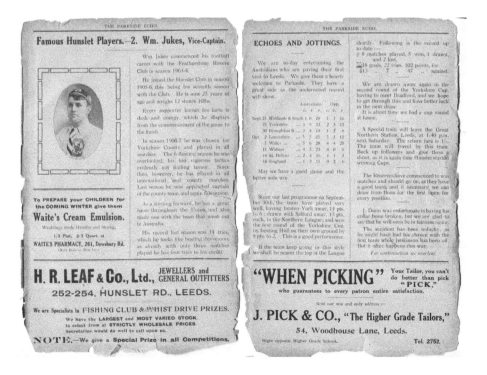

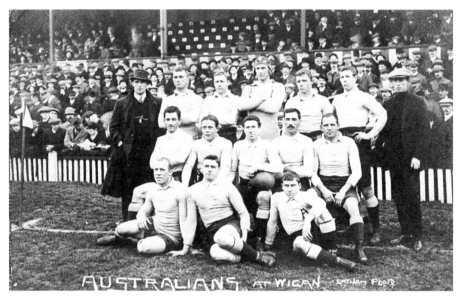

The Australian team before the game against Wigan at Central Park on 28 October 1911.

The match was witnessed by a crowd of 25,000, the highest attendance of the tour and far more than the collective attendance of the three test matches.

Both sides picked their strongest players and the game was an intense, determined struggle. The game soon developed into a contest dominated by strong defences, especially around the scrums, where the two wing forwards deployed by both sides restricted any open passing movements. Sharrock kicked a fine goal for Wigan and Hallett replied with a drop to see the teams change ends locked at 2-2. Midway through the second half Thomas gave Wigan a 4-2 lead with a successful penalty goal. With five minutes remaining Wigan finally created a gap in the tourists' defence with a movement described by the *Athletic News:* 'Thomas outwitted McKivatt in that he swerved to the left after a start to the right, and then Jenkins was equal to the remaining task, for when confronted by Fraser he served Leytham with a splendid pass and the try was safely made by the Wigan captain.' Sharrock failed at goal and the game ended with a 7-2 victory to Wigan.

The tourists performed their war cry before the first test match at St James's Park, Newcastle, on 8 November 1911.

A good crowd, estimated at around 6,000, braved a bitterly cold afternoon. The Northern Union side had an horrendous game, especially in defence, the *Leeds Mercury* commenting, 'The cardinal weakness on the

home side was the spotting and tackling, especially of the half-backs and centres.' They were particularly scornful of the tackling of the backs: 'The cases of clean tackling by the knees could be numbered on the fingers of one hand. If a Union defender was not clawing wildly at the air, he was doing the eyebrow clasp or the scalp enveloper.' The great Huddersfield centre Harold Wagstaff made his Anglo-Australian test match debut, but his form did little to enhance his reputation, one reporter commenting: 'Wagstaff could in fact do nothing right and has rarely been so impotent in an important match.' Fred Smith, the scrum half, was the only NU player to escape criticism, his performance described as 'indefatigable'. The real successes of the match were the tourists' forwards who finally mastered the art of NU scrummaging and in the loose attacked in units with clever short passing and constant backing-up. Playing behind a winning pack, captain Chris McKivatt had a superb game and was described by the *Leeds Mercury:* 'He is a born leader and a great half-back. He saw to it that Viv Farnsworth at stand-off was well plied with the ball, and the latter, in collaboration with Gilbert, was chiefly responsible for the confounding of Smith and Thomas.'

In the early minutes of the game the Union played well and seemed to be capable of a victory. A smart passing interchange by the half-backs led to a movement involving the full three-quarter line and ended when W. Davies crossed the line for a try, which Thomas converted with a long-range goal from the touch-line. Then a good try from Viv Farnsworth instigated a 15-minute offensive on the Union's line, during which the tourists took full advantage of the Union's pathetic defence and scored 19 points. At half-time the match was as good as over. The home side added a try and a goal, but the Australians were more than worthy 19-10 victors. The recriminations began immediately. However, the NU players were beaten by a better team of players whose objective was to win the Ashes. A major factor in the defeat was that the Union players were basically good, individual club players gathered together to oppose a squad who lived, ate and trained together.

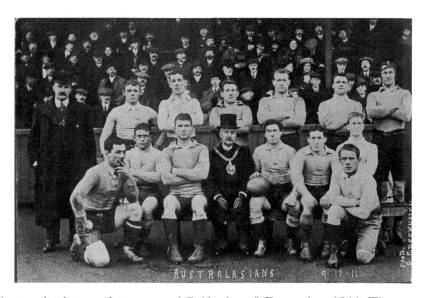

The tourists' team that opposed Salford on 9 December 1911. The mayor of Salford (middle of the front row) performed a ceremonial kick-off before the game and a crowd of 4,000 gathered at The Willows to witness the contest, during which the Australasians did not live up to expectations. The *Athletic News* commented, 'Candidly, the display of the tourists was one of the weakest I have seen.' The reporter praised the forwards' work in loose play and defence but criticised the usual poor play in gaining the ball from the scrums, commenting: 'the same old fault was apparent all through the game. Only at long intervals did the ball come through to McKivat.' The visitors opened the scoring with a try from Charles Russell. Salford soon equalised with a well-taken try by Mesley and the teams changed ends locked at 3-3. The tourists' backs began the second half with a series of clever combinations which the home side checked with some tremendous defensive play. Eventually a perfect pass from Chris McKivatt unlocked the midfield for Howard Hallett to score a try described by the *Athletic News:* 'Hallett completely bewildered half-a-dozen defenders with a grand run from the half-way line, finishing up over the line and grounding the ball close to the goalpost.' Arthur Francis failed with the conversion attempt and the game ended without a successful goal kick at 6-3 to the visitors.

The teams as published in the official programme for the Leeds v Australians match at Headingley on 6 January 1912. The fixture was expected to be a superb exhibition of Northern Union football and a great social event. However, the West Yorkshire climate managed to interfere and unleashed high winds, sleet and then a raging blizzard over the Headingley ground,

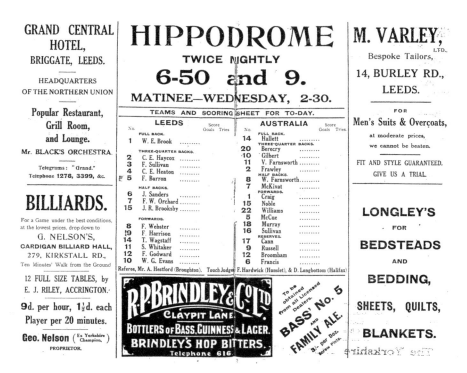

reducing the attendance to barely 1,000 and a gate of only £36. Despite the conditions the players kicked-off and played a competitive and interesting match. The tourists had to face the blizzard blowing directly into their faces in the first-half, yet they showed grit and perseverance and tackled well. Leeds had a powerful pack of forwards and, led by Fred Webster, soon gained the upper hand. Evans made a fine dribble and forced the tourists back. Then Sullivan fielded the ball in the open and passed to Heaton, who swerved to the right and transferred to Barron, who easily beat Frawley and scored behind the posts. The tourists hit back when Herb Gilbert set up a great platform with a straight run down the field. Hallett took advantage of the disorder in the Leeds defence and put in a short kick from which Gilbert crossed the line for a try. Minutes later Heaton snapped up a loose ball to score and at half-time the home side led 6-3. The Leeds forwards continued to play with 'unremitting zeal and energy'. However, with the wind at their backs the visitors soon took the lead when, following a successful penalty kick by Craig, Frawley sprinted over the line. The teams continued to battle the weather until the final whistle blew a welcome relief to everyone who had confronted the sleet, winds and eventually an insistent blizzard. The event was a financial disaster for everyone involved, the tourists and the Hunslet and Leeds clubs who had agreed to pool the takings from their tour matches.

The Batley side that defeated the tourists 13-5 on Saturday, 27 January 1912.

The line-up is, back row: Mr W. Kershaw Newsome (Secretary), Benny Laughlin, Jack Battersby, Mr William Shaw (President), Fred Hill, Harry Hodgson, William Fenton, Mr Arthur F.

Garner (trainer-coach). Middle: Walter Drummond, Joe Child, Fred Leek, Arthur Kitson, Tom Williams, James Debney. Front: John Moore, Willie Anderson, Eddie Ward, Jim Lyons.

The drama at Batley's Mount Pleasant ground started before the teams had taken to the field of play. A large crowd had gathered at the main entrance gates to the ground and refused to pay the shilling entrance fee. The situation was eventually solved when 3,000 had passed through the turnstiles and the game had started. It was decided to admit the protesters at six pence each. The rush for admission was then so great that the gates were torn from their frames, the police swept away, and hundreds entered the field without paying. When events eventually calmed down Batley soon began to attack the visitors' line and Moore scored from a clever pass by Laughlin. The 'Gallant Youths' of Batley continued to play superb football

and early in the second half Joe Child dropped a clever goal and then, from a clever dribble by Laughlin, Drummond beat Fraser and scored a fine try. The tourists replied with a try from Tom Cann which Arthur Francis converted. Batley's Tom Williams scored an unconverted try to give Batley a famous 13-5 victory. Late in the game Batley's Benny Laughlin was sent off for tripping and the tourists' forward Bob Williams was dismissed for insulting a touch-judge.

The Batley and Australian teams from the official card published for the game.

Chapter 4

1910 TO 1918

The teams for the 1910 Yorkshire Challenge Cup Final published in the official programme. The game was held at Headingley, Leeds. Therefore, the Leeds club produced the programme. The Wakefield side knew they were playing against some of the finest backs in the union and would have to keep the ball away from them as much as possible. Encouraged by an early two-point lead from a penalty kick by veteran full-back Metcalfe, Trinity's half-back Tommy Newbould found touch with a short kick near the Huddersfield line. The *Athletic News* commented: 'This was play with method, and the sequel was a smart try by G. Taylor, who appeared to be over the line before the opposing half-backs realised that the ball was out of the scrum.'

The *Leeds Mercury* also praised the Trinity forwards' performance: 'The Wakefield forwards were far too good for the big, non-working Huddersfield front rankers, and they showed even greater superiority in the loose. Their fast following up and sure tackling was the main factor in bringing about the victory of their side.'

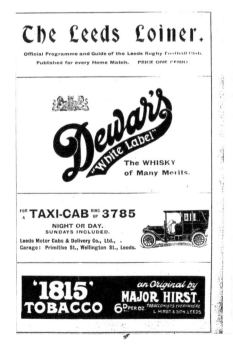

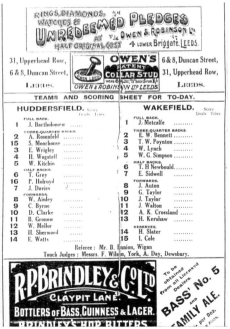

Wakefield struck again early in the second half when Bartholomew fumbled a pass and allowed Lynch to pick up and immediately transfer to Simpson who crossed for a try. Later New Zealander Edgar Wrigley kicked a penalty for Huddersfield and the game ended 8-2 to Trinity.

On their arrival in Wakefield at about 5.30pm the players with the cup and officials boarded a special tram which took them to their headquarters at the Alexander Hotel, Belle Vue. Following a 'capital' dinner and a host of speeches, the team with the cup visited the Empire Theatre and various hotels in the city.

Joseph Henry 'Jake' Blackmore, Hull Kingston Rovers.

Jake Blackmore was a Welsh Rugby Union forward who first played for Abertillery in 1902. He also briefly played for Tredegar and Blaina. Jake gained caps for Monmouthshire against both the South African and the Australian tourists. In 1909 he gained a full Welsh Test cap when he opposed England at Cardiff Arms Park. In 1910 Blackmore decided to join Hull Kingston Rovers. He made his debut for Rovers against Dewsbury on their infamous, sloping Crown Flatt pitch. The *Hull Daily Mail* commented: 'It was pleasing to note the improvement in Blackmore, who showed far better advantage than at practices. What he needs is a little more experience in the new game, and much more will be heard of this Welsh international.' Three months later Blackmore was selected for the Welsh Rugby League team in the game against England at Coventry. He played one more international for Wales against England at Ebbw Vale. Blackmore made 62 appearances for Hull Kingston Rovers, scoring 18 points.

Lawkholme Lane, Keighley, 1910.
This superb view captures the development of a small Northern Union ground. Grounds in the early days were usually simple fields without even basic attempts of enclosure. Gradually the fields were enclosed by picket

Keighley Football Field

fences, brick walls and iron railings and entrances were created to enable admission fees to be taken. The Keighley club had originally used farm trailers parked at the side of the pitch to give spectators an elevated view. This had progressed to the permanent elevated wooden structure built behind the posts illustrated in the photograph.

Ebbw Vale, 1910.
Ebbw Vale were the most successful of the Welsh clubs that joined the Northern Union. The doomed venture in South Wales had extremely poor support from the NU, apart from an ill-funded attempt to help with travelling expenses which were soon reduced to some clubs. The selfish

EBBW VALE R.F.C. 1910.

W James (Dir.)   J Matthews   D Williams   G Eustace   Malle   Bowen   G Da s (Man.)   M Price (T's.)
     G Hutchings   I Roberts   H Smith   C Jenkins   J Foley   W Higgi s   C Burgham
                    W Thomas   T Davies   L Llewellyn

ambitions of most of the big clubs in the heartlands of Lancashire and Yorkshire had little interest in clubs that involved increased travel costs and small gates. Like North West Lancashire and Cumberland, the opportunity to spread the Northern Union was unexploited. In early September 1912 Ebbw Vale announced that they would be unable to fulfil their fixtures and the club folded.

A newspaper illustration of the Warrington v Ebbw Vale match at Wilderspool, on 8 January 1910.

The Welsh team had recently had a run of six successive victories and were playing well. The *Athletic News* commented, 'One of the most improved teams in the Northern Union is undoubtedly Ebbw Vale, for they gave a delightful exposition at Wilderspool.' However, at Warrington they met a strong set of forwards who soon forced home the attack, and O'Malley scored a try in the first minute. Thomas added a penalty goal and then O'Malley scored a try following a run from the half-way line and at half-time the home team were leading 8-0. The visitors improved in the early stages of the second half, the *Yorkshire Post* recording, 'Clever work was done by Davies and Jenkins. Eventually Davies kicked a penalty goal, but the crowning effort was a try by Llewellyn, who, receiving on his quarter flag, raced through the home defence in splendid style.' Warrington fought back, and O'Malley and Brooks scored tries and Thomas kicked a goal. The game ended with a 16-8 victory to the home team.

The Wigan team before the Championship play-off game against Salford on 16 April 1910. Heavy rain and constant peals of thunder reduced the

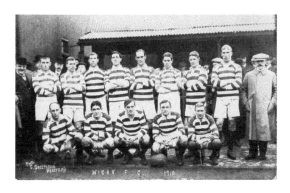

attendance at The Willows to 9,000 and the state of the pitch dictated play somewhat. De Francis opened the scoring following some clever footwork by the Wigan forwards shortly before half-time and following a similar forward rush by Salford Lomas was awarded an obstruction try when Price deliberately prevented him dropping on a ball he had dribbled over the line. Both sides had played well in the first half; however, the second half was totally different, the Athletic News commenting, 'The second half had not been going long when it was seen that Salford had lost nerve and that their opponents had gained confidence and Salford's fate was sealed. Their forwards were beaten for possession, their half-backs overplayed and their three-quarters out of work.' De Francis added another try, Leytham crossed for two, Jenkins one and Thomas kicked a goal, and Wigan were worthy 17-6 winners. Salford's captain Jim Lomas crossed for a try and had one disallowed. Lomas disputed the decision and at the end of the game the incident was reported by the Athletic News: 'The referee Mr Arnott Smith explained his decision to Lomas. Mr Smith understood that the straw behind the goal posts was the dead ball line and Lomas had grounded the leather just on the straw, but an inspection of the spot proved that the chalk line had not been reached and was some inches further away.' The Wigan players are, back row: unknown official, Whittaker, Thomas, Barton, De Francis, Seeling, Price, Silcock, Ramsdale with Jimmy Sharrock on the end in overcoat. Front row-Topping, Jenkins, Miller, Leytham, Jones.

The outer covers from *the Parkside Echo,* the Hunslet matchday programme from November 1911.

By 1910/11 several clubs were producing official matchday programmes for their home games. This scarce surviving Hunslet issue has many advertisements from mainly local companies as diverse as breweries, pubs, tailors, cobblers and cinemas. Also published are all the players names, shirt numbers and positions for both clubs. Each issue of *The Parkside Echo* also featured a pen picture of a player.

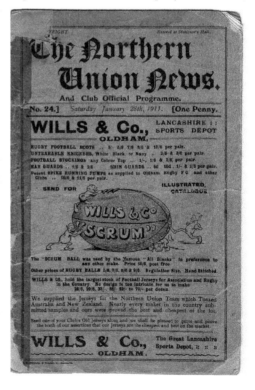

In 1911 the Northern Union were also publishing *The Northern Union News.* Clubs bought copies of the News then inserted their own four-page supplement with the names of the players. *The NU News* concentrated on news and articles covering the whole of the Union and had less advertisements and recorded full results of previous games and future fixtures. Surviving, intact copies are exceedingly rare.

Rochdale Hornets, Lancashire Cup winners, 1911.

Rochdale had been in existence for 40 years and their 1911 Lancashire Cup Final victory over Oldham was the club's first trophy. The Hornets started in a determined mood and their clever opening play surprised the 20,000-crowd at Wheater's Field, Broughton. Oldham played well at times but were let down by their three-quarters who fumbled far too many times when they were near the line. Rochdale's backs were far more meticulous. The *Athletic News* described them: 'The backs were more prominent in individual efforts than in combined movements, but even if their passing was slow, they were sure and made precious few mistakes. Each man supported the other, nothing was left to chance.' The Hornets held a 4-0 lead at half-time thanks to two penalty goals from Paddon. Early in the second half Oldham lost Arthur Anlezark when the Australian half-back had to retire with two broken ribs. Rochdale later increased their hold on the game when 'Schofield got possession from a scrum and, breaking away, sent a sharp inside pass to Turner, the forward took the ball beautifully and cut through and scored a brilliant try.' Three minutes from time Rochdale half-back Jones secured the Hornets victory when he dashed over from a scrum to make the result 12-5 to Rochdale.

On their return home the players and the cup mounted a waggonette and were escorted by mounted police and the Rochdale Old Band to their headquarters at the Albion Hotel. Thousands lined the station approach and principal streets to witness the procession.

Rochdale Hornets 'terrible six' forwards in 1911.

The six played a tremendous game against Oldham in the 1911 Lancashire Cup Final, the *Athletic News* commenting, 'Primarily one must give credit to the Rochdale forwards for the victory. The six played together with a will, were solid in the rush when the occasion demanded, and were clever in the loose when the Oldham scrummages failed to hold the ball.' On the far right of the front row is Walter 'Rattler' Roman who was an

Rochdale Hornets 'Terrible Six' –
Reading (left to right) – Back row: Jack Fitzsimmons, Jimmy Dearden
Front row: Ernest Jenkins, Alf Turner, Tommy Woods, Walter Roman

immensely strong player from Bridgwater, Somerset, who had signed for the Hornets in 1910. 'Rattler' toured Australia with the 1914 Lions. He later enlisted and was wounded by shrapnel in the hand, thigh and legs on the first day of the Battle of the Somme on 1 July 1916, his 36th birthday. He was evacuated from France on 5 July 1916 to an hospital in Cheltenham. Walter Roman died of his wounds on 28 July 1916 in Cheltenham, aged 36.

The Oldham team and officials at their Watersheddings ground, 1910/11.

The Oldham club had a highly successful season, winning the Lancashire Cup (the smaller trophy on the right) by defeating Swinton 4-3 at Broughton in early December 1910 and then defeating Wigan 20-7 in May 1911 to be crowned champions. A crowd of 15,000 witnessed the Championship Final at Wheater's Field, Broughton, where a clash of shirt colours led to Wigan playing in blue and white. Oldham in their red jerseys played a superb game from the kick-off, the *Athletic News* commenting, 'Oldham right well rose to the occasion and they were the side which commanded attention. Bustling and alert forwards, a pair of magnificent half-backs, a sound three-quarter line and a full-back who was not unduly worked.' The same reporter described their opponents: 'Wigan had no liking for their task. The backs and forwards have gone off their game, there was no support or understanding between the two divisions of the team, and they were as

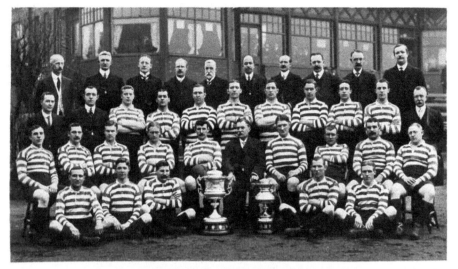

OLDHAM FOOTBALL CLUB. SEASON 1910-11.
FIRST TEAM & COMMITTEE.

a flock of sheep without a shepherd.' Oldham scored three brilliant tries. The first was described as follows: 'Gleave, diverting from orthodox tactics, heaved out a high, wide pass which appeared to catch Todd in two minds, the centre hesitated, and White was not slow to take full advantage. Out went the ball to W. Dixon on the wing, and although he appeared to be on the look out for someone to take the return pass, he beat the Wigan backs and on reaching Sharrock passed to White who crossed for a try.' The second Oldham try was the result of a typical charge by James Lomas. 'With that magnificent forceful run which has made him famous, he dashed at the waiting tacklers, one, two, and three wearers of the blue jersey, in vain attempted to bring him low and although numbers eventually told, Lomas kept the ball loose and White, who was handy, completed the try.'

James 'Jumbo' Lomas was one of the Northern Union's greatest players and in a career that lasted for 24 years he scored 2,005 club points. Jim was born in 1879 in Maryport, Cumberland, and played his early football for Maryport Rugby Union Club, switching when the club joined the Northern Union in 1898. His displays soon caught the attention of the scouts from West Yorkshire and young Lomas 'went south' to join Bramley in August 1900. Once again Jim's ability at centre was soon noticed and Salford paid the first £100 transfer fee to take him across the Pennines in 1901. 'Jumbo' quickly gained international honours and he captained the first Lions team to tour Australia in 1910. In the same year he was on the move again when ambitious Lancashire club Oldham created a new record transfer fee of £300 for his signature. James settled in well at Oldham and played a superb part in Oldham's Championship Final victory against Wigan. Lomas used his 5ft 7in and 13-and-a-half-stone frame to create panic in Wigan's defence with his bustling runs. His second try was a few moments of magic described by the *Athletic News:* 'The concluding try fittingly fell to Lomas and was an individual effort pure and simple. He intercepted the Wigan passing, ran to Sharrock, and then leaped over the full-back's arms as he attempted the tackle. Lomas continued his merry way, ran under the goal posts, coolly brought out the ball from the place and made his great effort worth five points.'

A rare image of the great James Lomas in action with the ball.

His display in the 1911 Championship Final was recorded by the *Athletic News:* 'With characteristic grit and determination the stalwart responded well to every call. His strong runs and his powerful dashes were unquestionably the main factor which led to the undoing of Wigan.'

A Hull Kingston Rovers' side from 1911. The canvas hoardings in the background served a double purpose, sited to prevent people from

'ROVER'S v HULL CHAMPIONSHIP 1911'

watching the game for free and painted adverts on the hoarding generated revenue. The canvas hoardings were commonplace at many grounds until they were gradually replaced by tall wooden fences and eventually brick and stone walls that totally enclosed grounds.

Eddie Guerin, of Hunslet.—One of the giants of the game. Usually gets what he wants—points!

A caricature of James Walter Guerin.

Walter Guerin joined Hunslet from Hartlepool Rugby Union Club in 1911. At over 6ft tall and around 16 stone, Guerin made a superb debut for Hunslet, scoring a try and a goal in the 25-5 defeat of Bramley. The *Leeds Mercury* described his try: 'Guerin scored the best try of the afternoon, culminating a strong and well-judged run three-parts the length of the field, in which he handed off three opponents, including that tenacious tackler Turton. His running action is deceptive, he looks slow, but he has a stride like the ship of the desert and takes a prodigious deal of catching. Guerin is a hard worker, a plucky tackler and a strong runner.' It was the beginning of a lengthy career that was to stretch to 1928. He played in every position for Hunslet and made just over 350 appearances and scored over 1,100 points. Walter was a popular figure in the city of Leeds and had the distinction of being one of only two men to lift 'Resista', the popular music hall act of the era.

Albert Victor Abbishaw, 1911. Albert Abbishaw was from Rothwell and played for Dewsbury. In this photograph he is wearing his Yorkshire cap having played loose-forward for Yorkshire against Cumberland at Salthouse, Millom, on Saturday 9 December 1911. In 1912 he was a member of the Dewsbury team that defeated Oldham to win the Challenge Cup.

The Hunslet and Hull FC teams prior to the inaugural Spring Bank Orphanage Cup charity match at the Boulevard, 10 September 1912. The game was also a normal league fixture and a good crowd of 10,000 gathered at the Boulevard, which included 150 children and their own brass band from the orphanage. A rumour that Hull would invite a weaker team to enable them to win the cup had circulated in the city in the days prior to the match. This was proved to be totally unfounded when Hunslet, a formidable team with top-four aspirations opposed the home side. The *Hull Daily Mail* described the play from both teams as: 'Fast, exciting and exhilarating.' Hull were 8-5 winners; all the points were scored in the first half. Smart work by Francis put Ned Rogers in under the posts and later Allen crossed the line following a forward rush. Later Hunslet's Harry Toft darted over from a scrum and Fred Farrar converted. At full time Hull were presented with the trophy and each player received a gold medal. The Hunslet players received silver medals.

Hull FC with the Spring Bank Orphanage Trophy in 1912.

Back row (left to right): Arthur Allen, George Connell, Ellis Clarkson and Alf Francis. Third row: Alf Grice, Jimmy Devereaux, Billy Holder, Tom Herridge, C. Cappleman and Alf Charlesworth (secretary). Seated: Tom Coates (trainer), George Cottrell, Frank Boylan, Ned Rogers, E. Schofield, A. Barrow, W. Wright (assistant trainer). In front: Gregor Rogers and G. Simpson.

Lew Bradley joined Wigan at the start of the 1911/12 season from Pontypool Rugby Union Club. Bradley had great pace and was a natural scorer of tries. In March 1914 he equalled Jimmy Leytham's record of tries scored in a match when he crossed for six tries in a home defeat of Rochdale Hornets. In total he scored 117 tries in 106 matches for Wigan. Lew was killed in action in France on 20 June 1918.

Herbert Richmond Gilbert at the Boulevard, Hull, in 1912.

In 1910 Hull FC were defeated in their third successive Challenge Cup Final and, eager for success, began a recruitment campaign to strengthen their squad. In 1912 they signed Australian Test footballer Bert Gilbert. Bert stood at 6ft and weighed 13-and-a-half stone and was an immensely strong and fast centre. The Australian soon fitted into the Hull team and made 114 appearances, scoring 173 points before he returned to Australia in 1916 to join South Sydney and then later Eastern Suburbs.

Australian Test footballer Steve Darmody signs his autograph for a fan at the Boulevard in 1912. Darmody signed for Hull at the same time as his 1911/12 Kangaroos tour teammate Bert Gilbert and the pair made their debut together on 5 September 1912. Darmody had played his early football on the wing or as a loose forward for South Sydney. At Hull he was a regular in the second row of the pack, but with his great pace he was equally at home as a centre. The Australian made 89 appearances for Hull, scoring 84 points.

The Australians Gilbert and Darmody were so overwhelmed by their welcome to Hull that they sent this note to the *Hull Daily Mail* thanking the people of the city.

The Australian players at Hull ready for a trip in a motor car in 1912. The three sat in the car are (left to right) Gilbert, Devereaux, who had signed for Hull in 1909, and Darmody. Gilbert, having moved during the prolonged exposure time, is also featured at the rear of the car.

A Hull team from the 1912/13 season. The full line of players has not survived. However, prominent are Tom Herridge (centre row),

Jack Harrison, Steve Darmody and far right Herb Gilbert (middle row) and Alf Francis (front on ground to the left).

A well-dressed crowd at Mount Pleasant, for the Batley v Dewsbury derby on 28 September 1912. A crowd of 13,000 witnessed Dewsbury defeat their local rivals 8-3 in a game described by the *Leeds Mercury* thus: 'The game was of a disappointing character, and for the most part play was of the scrambling, bustling order.' The section of the ground in the photograph was where the Short Stand was built in 1913.

Lucius Banks, Hunslet, 1912.

In 1912 Hunslet stunned the Northern Union world when they signed Lucius Banks, a black American cavalryman. Banks had been recommended by a Hunslet committee member who, while on business in New York, had seen him playing American football. He believed that the young athlete would somehow be able to sail the Atlantic Ocean and switch to Northern Union football. The Hunslet club backed the strange idea and bought Banks out of the American Army and found him a job with a local saddler. Banks made his debut for Hunslet in late January 1912 against York at Parkside. The *Yorkshire Post* commented: 'Although he was credited with a try, made for him by W. Batten, he was obviously strange in his new surroundings.'

Banks never settled in south Leeds. He struggled with the cold, damp weather, the food and the strange accents of his teammates and the people of Hunslet. He played a handful of games then went back to America.

Lucius Banks, Hunslet, 1912.
American Lucius Banks relaxes with some of his Hunslet teammates: (left to right) Jukes, Fowler, Banks, Randall and Wyburn. The Leeds newspapers were very hostile to Hunslet's new player, the *Yorkshire Evening Post* going as far as to comment under the unbelievable headline 'Hunslet's coloured coon' that the signing was a mere novelty and crowd pulling stunt and denied local talent a chance. The Hunslet club wrote to the newspaper to complain about the content of the article, but not the headline.

Hunslet team 1911/12.
The full line-up of this team is not recorded; however, some players are known: Back row, far left: Fred Smith, far right: Billy Jukes. Middle row with ball: Billy Batten, to the right: Herbert Place. In front Lucius Banks and Harry Toft.

The Coventry Northern Union Club, season 1911/12.
The Coventry Rugby Union Club were suspended from the ERU in October 1909 following a three-hour meeting during which club officials were 'interrogated' regarding travel and hotel expenses. Several committee members were found guilty of professionalism. The club had a problem: they

Coventry Northern Union Football Club, 1911/12 at The Butts. Back: A.Elton, J. Parkinson, T. Oldham, C. Piggott, H. Davis, J. Tomes, W. Hutt, E. Hutt Front: D. Benyon, R. Dakin, L. Beaver, P. Oldham (capt.) J. Houghton, T. Burdett, C. Carter

wanted to continue to play the handling code of football and made the decision to apply for membership of the Northern Union and were admitted in December 1910. The new club played their home games at The Butts, the home of the former Rugby Union club since 1880. Coventry struggled from the start. In the first season the club ended next to bottom in the league table and bottom in their final season in 1913.

The players for the Huddersfield and Wigan teams as published in the official programme for the Championship Final at Belle Vue on 3 May 1913. Huddersfield were the most famous and successful team in the Northern Union and by 1913 they were virtually at the pinnacle of their

achievements. The Huddersfield committee wanted the best players at Fartown and gathered together a group of gifted individuals from around the world.

Both teams had recruited well: Wigan had Leytham, Jenkins, Todd and Miller in their three-quarters, the great Johnny Thomas at half-back and expectations of a good open game were high. Huddersfield were described at the time as 'The Team of All Talents' and their backs, led by captain Harold Wagstaff, had taken the game to a new level, combining high speed and accurate passing to

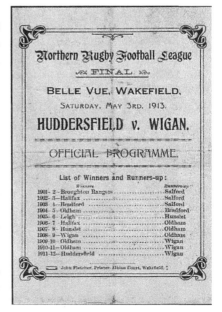

Northern Rugby Football League

⚡ FINAL ⚡

BELLE VUE, WAKEFIELD,

SATURDAY, MAY 3RD, 1913.

HUDDERSFIELD v. WIGAN.

OFFICIAL PROGRAMME.

List of Winners and Runners-up:

Winners	*Runners-up*
1901- 2 –Broughton Rangers	Salford
1902- 3 –Halifax	Salford
1903- 4 –Bradford	Salford
1904- 5 –Oldham	Bradford
1905- 6 –Leigh	Hunslet
1906- 7 –Halifax	Oldham
1907- 8 –Hunslet	Oldham
1908- 9 –Wigan	Oldham
1909-10 –Oldham	Wigan
1910-11–Oldham	Wigan
1911-12–Huddersfield	Wigan

John Fletcher, Printer, Albion Court, Wakefield.

execute movements that were said to have bewildered both opponents and the vast crowds that flocked to see them. The first half was a somewhat dull affair with both sides unable to produce any real rhythm in their methods. Eventually, the deadlock was broken when Wigan's Johnny Thomas kicked a goal from a 'mark' made by Bert Jenkins. The Fartowners hit back soon after when Clark charged by a poor kick by Sharrock and scored an unconverted try to give Huddersfield a slender one-point advantage. From the start of the second half Huddersfield took control of the game through their forwards: 'The six sturdy men whilst doing their whack in the scrummages, handled the ball with consummate ability in the loose.' With the forwards gaining most of the ball from the scrums, half-backs Grey and Davies soon eclipsed the Wigan pair of Gleave and Thomas and swiftly transferred possession to the three-quarters. The *Athletic News* reported, 'Wigan were no match in the backs for the superior pace and masterly combination of Davies, Wagstaff, Gleeson and Moorhouse.' Huddersfield, now in almost complete control, added more points with tries from Grey, Moorhouse, Rosenfeld (2) and two more from Clark to complete his hat-trick and four goals from full-back Major Holland to give them a 29-2 victory. Times were changing and the Huddersfield players were conveyed back to the George Hotel by a motor coach. Persistent heavy rain reduced the crowds gathering to welcome the team home. However, the cup and team still appeared at the windows of the George Hotel for the ones who braved the weather.

Harold Wagstaff, 'The Prince of Centres.'
In November 1906 Huddersfield signed 15-year-old Harold Wagstaff from Underbank, a small village above Holmfirth. Wagstaff's age caused some concern at Fartown, one critic writing, 'We want men not boys.' However, this was soon answered with, 'If he's good enough he's old enough.' Wagstaff was a clever young man and a great student of the game and its methods of play. Young 'Waggy' quickly developed into one of the finest exponents of centre play the game had seen, and his methods soon earned him his nickname. As captain of the team his ideas were simple. Players were discouraged from punting the ball at the opposition and encouraged to pass the ball. The forwards were also encouraged to interchange with the backs. He also developed the 'reverse pass', often called scientific obstruction, a

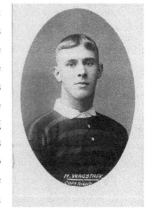

move which when first introduced simply bamboozled the opposition. Above all, Waggy moulded his team of brilliant individuals into a well-oiled working machine built on team work and support for one another. The 'Team of All Talents' finally reached the peak of perfection in the 1914/15 season when the Fartowners won All Four Cups, including a 35-2 trouncing of Leeds in the Championship play-off final at Belle Vue, Wakefield. Harold Wagstaff made 436 appearances for Huddersfield and scored 549 points.

A Bradford Northern team at their Birch Lane ground in 1913. Northern had moved to Birch Lane from Greenfield Stadium in 1908. The players are, back row 4th from left McEwan, middle row (left to right): Harry Feather, John Haley, Crispen Carter, Harold James Ruck and George Hall. Front row: Norman Wilby, Harry Schofield, Joe Winterburn, J. B. Simmons, W. H. Irvine, F. Wilson and W. H. Mitchell.

George Crabtree, the Swinton full-back, caricatured as fiddling with the ball too much in a game for the Lions in 1913. Crabtree was signed by Swinton in 1912 following his superb play in a workshops competition organised by the club. The young full-back made just nine appearances for Swinton, his last against Wigan on 13 December 1913. At the outbreak of the First World War he enlisted in the Lancashire Fusiliers. George Crabtree was killed in action at Gore in France on 20 April 1917. He was 23 years old.

Crabtree (Swinton's full-back) fiddled with the ball too much last Saturday.

The Swinton side which opposed Broughton Rangers on 13 September 1913. The game was witnessed by an estimated 8,000 and officially opened Rangers' new home, The Cliff, situated on land between the River Irwell and Lower Broughton Road, Higher Broughton. Formed in 1877 by Robert Seddon, Broughton Rangers first played on Peel Park, Walness Lane, and in 1895/96 the club moved to Wheater's Field, a ground said to be 'totally devoid of grass.' They moved to The Cliff when the landlord of Wheater's Field increased the rent by 25 per cent. The new ground was described as a modern playing enclosure with up-to-date rooms for players, visitors and officials. The visitors from Swinton spoilt the party when they defeated their hosts 14-0. Broughton had a big heavy pack, and although they secured the ball far more than the visitors they rarely got clean away, their heavy, cumbersome forwards beaten by the speed in which the more nimble Swinton men broke up. The *Athletic News* commented on the events as follows: 'Swinton played the modern game; Broughton mainly worked on old, worn out methods, and the tactics of head and hands deservedly triumphed.' Swinton's points were scored by Matt Ryder who kicked four goals, his first successful kick being the first points recorded at The Cliff. Dick Price and Dick Cullis each scored a try.

Batley with the Yorkshire Cup, 1912.

Back row (left to right): Eddie Ward, Tom Parker, Fred Leek and James Debney. Middle: Jim Gath, Benny Laughlin, 'Billy' Fenton, Arthur Kitson

(Captain), Harry Hodgson, Fred Hill and Arthur Garner (trainer-coach). Front: Clem Garforth, Jack Brooksby, Jack Battersby, Jim Lyons, Jack Tindall, Walter Drummond and J. W. Lockwood.

A good crowd of 16,000 gathered at Headingley to watch an extremely poor game described as 'one long, glaring exhibition of how the game should not be played.' The strange, archaic tactics implemented by Hull half-back Billy Anderson were blamed for the quality of play. Anderson had a fine strong pack of forwards who gave him almost constant control of the ball. However, Anderson rarely opened play by passing to his backs and constantly gave the ball to Batley when he launched short kicks from the rear of the scrum. In the words of the *Leeds Mercury*, 'With equal persistency did Anderson show an utter disregard for anyone but himself. He appeared to imagine that Hull had only one back, and that was he.' The *Hull Daily Mail,* faithful supporters of Northern Union football and Hull FC, commented: 'Gilbert and Francis fairly begged for chances. Whatever is the use of playing the clever Australian and the nippy young Welshman if they are not to receive a decent share of the ball.' *The Mail* also with tongue in cheek suggested that the Hull directors post the following notice at the Boulevard: 'An official notice, players indulging in silly kicking, especially in matches away from the Boulevard, will be liable to dismissal.'

Batley were 17-3 winners over Hull with tries from Tindall (2) and Brooksby and goals from Lyons, Garforth and Brooksby with two.

The Hunslet team that defeated Leeds 13-8 in the Lazenby Cup game at Parkside on 15 March 1913. The trophy had been donated in 1912 as a prize for the annual charity match between the clubs. A share of the gate takings was used to rent grounds for junior sides in Leeds. A good crowd of 8,000 gathered to watch the local derby, expecting the cross-city rivals to provide a keen game. Unfortunately, the game was marred by its excessive keenness and referee Dickinson found it necessary to send-off five players. The first to go were Jukes and Ward for fighting. Shortly before half-time, Dinny Campbell scored a brilliant, if somewhat lucky, try when the Australian centre broke down the middle of the field and 'seeing no hope of bursting through, Campbell kicked, and the ball hit an upright and bounced back. Campbell had followed his kick and caught the ball to cross for a try.' The *Yorkshire Evening Post* recorded the bizarre incidents following the try: 'Haycox kicked the goal but it was only after the third attempt. It appeared that on the first attempt the Hunslet players were not on the goal line and the players showed signs of stupidity in refusing to go back. Albert Goldthorpe, the Hunslet vice chairman, went on to the

field to tell the players to obey the referee's instructions. Referee Dickenson then allowed Haycox two more attempts.' At half-time committee members from both clubs lectured the players on their conduct. The harsh words had little effect for in the second half Davies from Leeds and Smales of Hunslet were dismissed for fighting and later Fred Webster for punching Harry Toft. Fred Smith (2) and Smalley scored tries for Hunslet and Guerin and Toft kicked goals. For Leeds, Ganley and Campbell scored tries and Haycox kicked a goal.

The line-up for the Leeds v Coventry game at Headingley on 14 March 1913. Witnessed by a crowd of 4,000, Leeds defeated Coventry 102-0. From the kick-off the visitors put up extraordinarily little resistance to the constant attacks by Leeds and the home side simply did as they pleased. At half-time, with the score at 39-0, the game as a contest was over. In

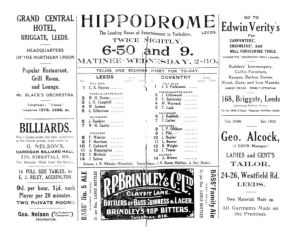

the second half Coventry's play 'was miserably weak throughout with only Parkinson, Ruddick and Cash of note. The others played limply and aimlessly.' Dinny Campbell, the Leeds captain, began to direct the ball at players who had not scored tries and when 11 players had scored tries, he gave Haycox and Sanders the chance to kick goals. Both players were soon on the score sheet and the record of every player from a team scoring points was created. Campbell, with help from Ganley and Sanders, was always the architect of the victory, calmly directing play. At full-time Leeds had scored 24 tries and 15 goals, the 102 points a then record score at Headingley. The scorers were: Tries: Webster (8), Davies (4), Campbell (3), Jarman (2) Rimmington, Godward, Mirfield, Gilbertson, Ganley, Harrison and Sutton. Goals: Ganley (9), Haycox (2), Sanders, Webster, Sutton, and Campbell.

John Dennison 'Dinny' Campbell. Dinny Campbell was an Australian Rugby Union centre who gained three international caps. In 1910 Dinny switched codes of football and played alongside Dally Messenger in the Eastern Suburbs Rugby League team. In 1912 Campbell made the decision to join Leeds Northern Union Club and made his debut against Keighley at Headingley on 14 September 1912. Campbell did little to impress the Headingley crowd. The *Yorkshire Post* commented: 'Unfortunately the game did not run his way. Moreover, he was badly neglected by his colleagues, and he also received close attention from his opponents.' The fact that Campbell was neglected was probably because the Leeds backs at the time were considered a formation of individuals. Campbell eventually became one of the Leeds club's finest players and his clever, thoughtful method of play helped to lay the foundations of a great side. Dinny made 258 appearances and scored 414 points for Leeds before returning to Australia.

KINGSTON ROVERS N.U.F.C. 1913-14

Hull Kingston Rovers team, 1913/14. Rovers had finished sixth in the league table and defeated Millom 62-0 in the first round of the Challenge Cup before being knocked out 2-17 at home by Huddersfield. Early in the season the club had signed Tommy McGiever from Leigh, who went on to make 157 appearances, scoring 78 points.

Rochdale Hornets, 1913/14. The Hornets had a good season, winning the Lancashire Cup for the second time when they defeated Wigan at Weaste, Salford. A reduced crowd of 4,000 gathered to witness a struggle on a very heavy pitch that hampered any serious attempts at open play. Wigan's

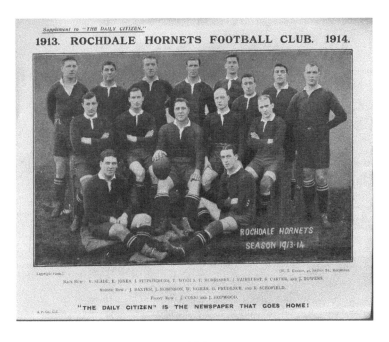

Supplement to "THE DAILY CITIZEN."

1913. ROCHDALE HORNETS FOOTBALL CLUB. 1914.

ROCHDALE HORNETS
SEASON 1913-14

"THE DAILY CITIZEN" IS THE NEWSPAPER THAT GOES HOME!

Welsh half-back Johnny Thomas opened the scoring with a first-half penalty goal. In the second half the Hornets mastered the conditions and their forwards constantly pressed the Wigan line, and eventually half-back Jones rushed over the line for a try. It was the only score of the half and at full-time Rochdale were worthy winners of the Lancashire Cup.

In early April 1913 Hull FC ended weeks of speculation and rumour when they paid Hunslet a record transfer fee of £600 for Billy Batten and agreed to pay him an outstanding £14 a week. Batten was one of the game's early stars. An exceptionally strong centre or winger, Batten was deadly in both attack and defence. Born in Kinsley, a small mining village near Hemsworth, he played his first football for Kinsley and Ackworth United before signing for Hunslet late in the 1906/07 season. The 18-year-old soon fitted into the Hunslet team and he was a regular first-team player during the 1907/08 season when the south Leeds club became the first club to win All Four Cups. Billy made

41 appearances and was the club's leading try scorer with 21 touch downs. It was during the All Four Cups season that Billy developed the famous Batten leap. Interviewed in 1913, he described the play during a mid-week game against Leeds: 'I had run until I got up to Frank Young and another Leeds player near the line and as there was nothing for it, I dived clean over the top of them and scored.' Hunslet were reluctant to sell Batten but were constantly struggling financially and there was another factor in the transfer which the club explained to their followers in an copy of the matchday programme, *the Parkside Echo*, in early April: 'When a man deliberately tells you that he will not don another jersey for Hunslet as long

as he lives, something has to be done. The committee would have been open to blame had they made no move in the matter, which would have no doubt ended in him joining the soccer code, and the club not receiving a halfpenny benefit. The soccer club was Manchester United, who had offered Batten £2 a week to join their squad.

On 12 April 1913 8,000 assembled to witness Batten make his debut for Hull against Keighley at the Boulevard. Hull trounced the West Yorkshire side 40-3 and Batten had a superb game, scoring three tries and creating two more and inspiring his new teammates to their highest score of the season. The *Athletic News* commented, 'Batten's strength carried him to success where many others would have failed. He helped to make Harrison a more formidable wing man and although Gilbert was often prominent, Batten was the most efficient performer in the Hull third line.' It was to be the start of a long partnership between Batten and the Hull Football Club and indeed the city of Kingston Upon Hull. Billy became the darling of the Boulevard crowd and posters advertising home games often had 'Batten will play' added to them. Batten made his final appearance for Hull away to Bramley on 5 April 1924. He had played 226 games and scored 269 points for Hull.

Billy Batten and his son at the Boulevard, Hull, in 1913.

The Wakefield Trinity team that defeated Keighley 10-0 at Belle Vue on 7 February 1914. A crowd of 2,000 witnessed a dour forward-dominated struggle, Tommy Newbould and Benjamin Johnson scoring tries. The players are, back row (left to right): John Abbott, John Mills, Arthur Dixon, A. K. Crossland, Tommy Poynton, Tommy Newbould, George Bolton. Front row: Jonathon Parkin, Billy Lynch, Ernest Parkin, Arthur Burton, Herbert Kershaw, Billie Beatie, Benjamin Johnson, Leonard Land.

Jonathon 'Jonty' Parkin was born at Sharlston, Wakefield, on 5 November 1894. Jonty played his early football at stand-off with the local Sharlston team. He signed for Wakefield Trinity in early April 1913 aged 18, and made his debut for the 'Dreadnoughts' in the 7-6 win against Bradford Northern at their Birch Lane Ground on 19 April 1913. Conditions in Bradford were hardly suited for the young half-back's style of play, the ground was in a bad condition and a strong cross-wind swept diagonally across the field. Aided by the wind, Northern played well in the first half and Kirton and Wilby created chances, but the three-quarters' finishing was poor. Trinity took control of the game in the second half and young Jonty excelled. One report stated, 'Parkin played especially well, he was always to the front with

smart dribbling and making openings for his side.' It was an excellent start to his career with Trinity, during which he made 349 appearances and scored 476 points.

Albert Aaron Rosenfeld was one of the greatest try-scorers the game has ever seen. Born in Sydney in 1885, 'Rozzy' played his early football for New South Wales and Eastern Suburbs in the newly established Australian Rugby League. He was a member of the first Australian tour of 1908/09 and in 1909 signed for Huddersfield. Rosenfeld had played in the stand-off position in his early years, but Huddersfield switched him to right wing for the 1910/11 season. Rozzy was a natural on the flank, with his great pace and powerful build (he stood at 5ft 5in and weighed just under 12 stone) created havoc in opposing defences and he crossed for 38 tries. The following season he was a regular and valuable member of the Huddersfield team that was playing some of the finest football the game has ever witnessed and he went over for 78 tries, a new record. During the 1913/14 season Albert smashed his own record and scored 80 tries, an incredible achievement and a record that still stands today. Albert scored 56 tries during Huddersfield's All Four Cups season of 1914/15 and then joined the ASC during World War One, where he served time in Mesopotamia (now Iraq).

A Wigan 'A' team, 1914.

Back row (left to right): Mr L. Pennington, Whalley, Sherrington, Melling, Banks, Molloy, Litherland, Blan. Middle row: Whittaker, Miller, Williams, Price, Curwen, Jolley. Front row: Guy, Hesketh.

A Salford team from the 1913/14 season.

Salford, who had struggled financially the previous year, had a good season and created a huge shock when they defeated Huddersfield in the Championship Play-Off Final at Headingley on 25 April. The L & NW Railway Company provided a series of special excursion trains offering third-class day return tickets to Leeds New Station from Patricroft, Eccles, Weaste, Seedley and Ordsall Lane for three shillings and three pence and from Manchester Exchange for three shillings. Hundreds took advantage and the crowd was an estimated 10,000. At Headingley Huddersfield started in style when the ubiquitous Harold Wagstaff slipped a superb pass to Tommy Gleeson who crossed for an unconverted try. Salford hit back, and following a series of scrums close to the Huddersfield line Charlie Rees crossed in the corner. Bernard Mesley, from an acute angle and against a strong wind, kicked a brilliant conversion that would prove to be the match winner. The Fartowners stormed the Salford line in the final ten minutes but a superb Salford defence and a series of crucial dropped passes denied them. With minutes left Wagstaff declined a penalty attempt and elected to force a victory. Salford held on and their brave defensive play gave them a well-fought famous victory. The triumphant Salfordians returned home by train and thousands were waiting at the Exchange Station, Manchester, when their train, which was an hour late, steamed into the station. The players and the cup then transferred to a charabanc, which led by the Hesary National Brass Band, toured Salford en route to Weaste.

John 'Jack' Harrison, Hull FC, 1914.

Jack Harrison was born in Hull in November 1890. He played his early football for St John's College, York. He then signed for York NU and played games for them during the 1911/12 season. Jack returned to Hull in September 1912 and signed for Hull FC, making his debut on 5 September 1912. During the 1913/14 season he played on the wing alongside Billy Batten and scored a club-record 52 tries. Jack made 116 appearances for the club, scoring 106 tries.

In 1915 Harrison joined the army and was commissioned as a second lieutenant in the East Yorkshire Regiment. On 25 February 1917 he led a patrol into no-man's land and was awarded the Military Cross for 'conspicuous gallantry and devotion to duty.'

On 3 May 1917 he was killed in action at Oppy Wood, Pas-De-Calais. Jack was posthumously awarded the Victoria Cross.

Crown Flatt, Dewsbury.

The laying of the foundation stone for the first-ever covered stand at the ground on 8ᵗʰ August 1914. The barrel-roofed stand seated 1,300 with a standing paddock for 2,000.

A Bramley team group in 1914. There are no records of the players' names.

Alfred 'Alf' Francis and his Hull FC teammates at Paragon Station, 1914. Alf had been picked to tour Australia with the NU Lions squad for their second visit to Australia and New Zealand and his teammates were at the station to wish him luck for his momentous journey. Francis played his early football with South Wales club Treherbert, one of a handful of Welsh Rugby Union Clubs that joined the Northern Union. They joined the NU in 1908 and left in April 1910. Francis joined Hull FC in September 1910 and became a first-team regular on the wing, scoring a try in the 1914 Challenge Cup Final win over Wakefield Trinity at Halifax in 1914. 'Alf' Francis made 247 appearances for Hull, scoring 166 tries.

A Leeds team at Salford, 1914.

Back row (left to right): Fred Mirfield, Billy Ward, Fred Webster, Fred Godward, W.G. Evans.

Front row: Lawrence Beecroft, W. H. Davies, Daniel Lewis, Samuel Jarman, Fred Harrison.

In front: Jimmy Sanders and Herbert Ganley.

Salford team group, 1915.

The American boxer Jack Johnson visits Crown Flatt, Dewsbury, for the home game against York on 20 November 1915. Johnson is accompanied by his wife Lucille. The pair had fled America when Jack was charged under the Mann Act for transporting a woman across state lines for immoral purposes. The racist authorities had hounded the black heavyweight boxing champion for years.

The couple were in Dewsbury to make an appearance at the Empire Theatre.

Two thousand people witnessed Dewsbury trounce York 72-0, with Jonty Parkin scoring four tries and Rhodes kicking 12 goals.

Bramley, 1916. The players are posing outside the Barley Mow pub, their headquarters at the time.

Dewsbury, 1916. The Northern Union announced that from 1915 all the major competitions would cease for the duration of the war. However, clubs were allowed to arrange friendly games, but the payment of players

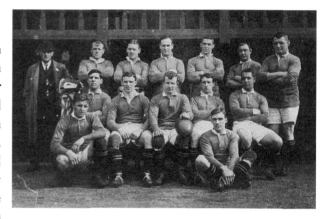

was banned. They did, however, allow expenses of two shillings and six pence to provide players with a tea. Some newspapers published results and compiled unofficial league tables. In 1916 Dewsbury declared themselves unofficial champions. The Crown Flatt-based club had taken full advantage of the suspension of players' registrations and recruited players from clubs that had closed during the war. This photograph features several 'guest 'players who assisted the club in 1916.

Back row (left to right): J. Davies trainer, Arthur Burton, Billy Rhodes, A Dixon, Percy Brown, Kershaw (Wakefield), Crosland (Wakefield). Front row: Billy Batten (Hull), Joe Lyman, T. Price, Farrar, Reynar Robertshaw, Kneeling Jonty Parkin and E. Rogers.

Leigh, 1916.

A 1916 poster for a charity game held at Foulby, Wakefield.

Billy Lynch made his début for Wakefield Trinity during September 1907. He played centre or winger and made 258 appearances, scoring 71 tries and 217 points for Trinity. On retirement from playing, Billy Lynch was the landlord of the Windmill Inn, Doncaster Road, Foulby, and on 22 March 1916 he arranged a rugby league match for the benefit of Leonard Hewitt from Hemsworth who had been incapacitated while in training with His Majesty's forces. The teams were captained by Billy Batten and Billy Lynch.

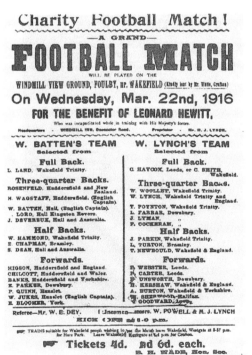

Chapter 5

THE NORTHERN RUGBY FOOTBALL UNION CHALLENGE CUP COMPETITION 1897 TO 1922

The Northern Rugby Football Union Challenge Cup competition was initiated at a NU committee meeting on 5 March 1896, setting out the following rules: 'All clubs in membership of the NU be eligible to join, all cup-tie gates up to semi-final be equally divided between the two competing clubs. That in the semi-final and final ties the gate be divided into three equal portions; one-third to each of the competing Clubs and the remaining third to the Northern Union.'

The Union commissioned Fattorini Silver Smiths of Bradford to design the trophy. Fattorini regularly outsourced more specialised items of the manufacturing process, such as the intricate skill of 'silver chasing,' to other companies. They did this for the Challenge Cup, and the trophy was manufactured in the Northern Quarter of Manchester by Messrs Lloyd, Paine and Amiel. Fattorini did, however, make the gold and silver medals for the winners and runners-up.

The draw for the first Challenge Cup competition was made on 3 September 1896, with 52 clubs involved. The first-round matches took place on 20

152

March 1897 and the competition then continued with rounds which were played on consecutive Saturdays until Batley and St Helens contested the first final tie at Headingley Stadium on 24 April 1897. The inaugural Challenge Cup Final was a well-organised, remarkable success. The NU committee held a meeting at the Mitre Hotel, Leeds, their headquarters for the day, then hosted a luncheon at Brayshay's Restaurant on Bond Street. After lunch, a fleet of horse-drawn carriages collected the party and the procession, with the Challenge Cup occupying a prominent position at the head of the parade, made their way through streets thronged with supporters from both teams. The crowds were so dense on the roads around the ground that mounted police were deployed to clear a path for the parade. Headingley was packed with 13,492 fans awaiting the kick-off. St Helens started and the strong Batley forwards soon began a series of rushes and dribbles towards the Saints' line, and after five minutes' play Joe Oakland dropped a clever goal directly from a scrum.

Play then moved to the Batley line where some openings made by St Helens failed when the final transfers were fumbled. Batley attacked again and Davies, collecting from a scrum, launched a cross-kick which John Goodall collected and he dashed over for a try to give Batley a 7-0 lead at half-time. In the second half St Helens scored a superb try which the *Liverpool Mercury* described: 'Doherty gained possession, and, after a capital run to the centre, passed to Traynor, who continued the forward movement, and, dodging several opponents and handing off others, in splendid style,

completed a try, amid the most demonstrative enthusiasm.' Shortly before full-time, Munns scored a try for Batley to give the Gallant Youths a 10-3 victory. The trophy was presented by Mrs Waller, the wife of the president of the Union.

John B. Goodall, the Batley captain and centre, who scored the first try in the final, with the Challenge Cup at Mount Pleasant.

Batley with the Challenge Cup at their Mount Pleasant Ground in 1897.

Back row: Jim Gath, John T. 'Paudie' Munns, Fred Lowrie, Tom Wilby, John B. Goodall (captain) behind cup, Charlie Stubley, Harry Goodall, Richard Barraclough and Fred Fisher.

Middle row: Mark Shackleton, Joe Oakland, Bob Spurr and Jim Littlewood.

Front row: Mr Joe Wilson (trainer-coach), Joe Naylor, Arthur Garner, Ike Shaw, George Main and Mr Fred Bennett (trainer-coach). Missing from the photo are Wattie Davies & Dai Fitzgerald.

The Batley players and officials with the cup. Back row: Mr William Cairns (assistant trainer), Mr Joe Wilson (trainer), Mr Mark Shackleton (trainer). Second back row: Frank Hollingworth, 'Bob' Spurr, Dai Fitzgerald, Ike Carroll, Pat Judge, Jim Midgley. Second row: Fred 'Ted' Fozzard, George Main, Jack Rogers, Joe Oakland (captain), Frederic Wilfrid Hoyle Wilf

Auty, Richard Lloyd, Joe Wolstenholme. Front row: Charlie Stubley, Wattie Davies, Arthur Garner, John B. Goodall.

Back row : (officials) Mr Harry Brook (treasurer), Mr William R. Binns (finance secretary), Mr Joe Wilson (trainer), Mr William G. Isherwood (vice-president), Mr David Fox Burnley (president), Mr James Sheard ('reporter' representative), Mr Fred Bennett (trainer), Mr James Goodall (vice-president), Mr William H. Shaw (correspondence secretary). Third row: George Main, Tom Wilby, Fred Fisher, Jim Gath, Fred Lowrie, Jim Littlewood, John T. 'Paudie' Munns, Harry Goodall, Joe Naylor. Second row: Dai Fitzgerald, Arthur Garner, John B. Goodall (captain), Joe Oakland, 'Bob' Spurr. Front row: Richard Barraclough, Herbert Hallas, Charlie Stubley, 'Wattie' Davies, Mark Shackleton, Ike Shaw.

As soon as the result at Headingley was known, 'telephone, telegraph and carrier pigeon' spread the news to Batley. Crowds of people from surrounding districts flocked to the town centre to witness the cup come to Batley. Trade was at a standstill when the crowds made their way to the station approaches. Then at 7.45pm the explosions of 100 fog signals laid on the tracks heralded the arrival of the team and the cup. 'On the appearance of the Batley captain J. B. Goodall, who held the cup aloft, there was tremendous cheering from the thousands who had assembled in and near the station yard.' The police eventually cleared a way for the party to board two horse-drawn waggonettes.

With the Batley Old Band leading, a procession was formed (which included the Corporation Fire Brigade, Queen St Mills Brigade and members of the Batley Working Men's Club with the silver trophy from the West Riding Billiard League they had won). The parade toured the town, stopping at the Market Place, 'where a potato roasting machine was prominent', and the town hall where the mayor welcomed the players. It eventually reached their headquarters at the Royal Hotel, where the players retired to the billiards room and the celebrations continued when the cup was filled with champagne.

Batley players and officials with the Challenge Cup in 1898.

Mr William H. Shaw (correspondence secretary), Mr Harry Brook (treasurer), Mr William G. Isherwood (vice-president), Mr David Fox Burnley (president), Mr James Goodall (vice-president) and Mr Ben Scott (financial secretary). Third row (left to right): Mr Joe Wilson (trainer-coach), Fred Fisher, Jim Phillips, Dai Fitzgerald, Mark Shackleton, Jim Gath, 'Jack' Rogers, John T. 'Paudie' Munns, Mr James Sheard (reporter representative) and Mr Fred Bennett (trainer-coach). Second row: Alfred

Fenton, 'Bob' Spurr, Arthur Garner, John B. Goodall (captain), Joe Oakland and Harry Goodall. Front row: Fred 'Ted' Fozzard, 'Wattie' Davies, Charlie Stubley and George Main.

The Challenge Cup holders faced Bradford, who had not been beaten since early December. Thousands of football enthusiasts converged on the Headingley ground. The travel arrangements had been well-planned to prevent the large crowds congregating on the central stations. With the Midland Railway routing their cheap day excursions to Kirkstall Station and the Great Northern to Headingley, tram and omnibus services were extended. Facilities at the ground had also been improved, with additional turnstiles, and on the terraces special barriers had been erected to prevent crowd swaying. In and around the ground hawkers were selling pork pies, chocolate and Doncaster butterscotch. Shortly before the teams entered the playing field, a series of large paper balloons, each bearing adverts for jam and soap, were released over the ground. A huge roar from the record crowd of 27,941 erupted when the game kicked-off. Bradford started well and were soon near the Batley line. The Gallant Youths defended well, and their forwards gradually took control of the game and took the lead when Wattie Davies dropped a goal. Bradford soon tired and in the final ten minutes were a beaten and deflated side. Batley's John Goodall crashed over for a try and minutes later dropped a smart goal to complete the scoring and give Batley a 7-0 victory and the cup again. The *Hull Daily Mail* commented, 'the Bradford forwards were hopelessly thrashed, and it was to their own front rank that Batley owe their victory. Batley's clever spotting was a feature in a splendid game.' The *Bradford Daily Telegraph* commented, 'it was in open footwork where the Gallant Youths had the pull. Gath, Shackleton and Fisher were almost invincible in that department.'

By 1899 the Challenge Cup competition had become a remarkable success, with northern-based newspapers fuelling the interest with superb coverage. This illustration from the *Athletic News* depicts the Yorkshire v Lancashire aspect of the 1899 final between Hunslet and Oldham.

Oldham with the Challenge Cup in 1899.

The Hunslet v Oldham 1899 final was held at Fallowfield Stadium. The home of the Manchester Athletic Club, it was an expansive enclosure with a good playing surface but with poor vantage points. This may have been a factor in the reduced attendance of 15,762. Oldham were generally regarded as one of the best teams in Lancashire, with a strong mobile pack and a set of clever, skilful backs. Hunslet began the game by using their strong heavy forwards in rushes and dribbling movements. The tactics worked well and with Walter Goldthorpe scoring a try and his older brother Albert kicking three goals, at half-time the Parksiders had a 9-5 lead. In the second half Oldham's lighter forwards took control of the game, and with the Hunslet pack noticeably struggling, they moved forward Owen Walsh to the backs to try to stem the Oldham attack. The *Leeds Mercury* commented, 'a confession of inferiority and a conspicuous failure.' Walsh later returned to his place in the forwards when Walter Goldthorpe retired with a broken collar bone. In the final quarter of the game Williams (2), Moffatt, and Joe Lees crossed for tries to give Oldham a 19-9 victory and the distinction of being the first Lancashire

side to win the cup. Following the presentation of the cup, the Oldham players and officials dined at the Exchange Hotel, Manchester. The party was then driven to their Oldham headquarters, the Red Lion Hotel, Mumps. The Red Lion was packed with supporters, with hundreds more outside who 'cheered the players when they appeared at an upper window where the cup was filled with champagne and emptied repeatedly,' and the crowds remained, cheering outside the hotel until midnight. Not all the supporters were honest that Saturday night, especially Anne Shaw, a well-dressed young woman who on Monday morning was charged at Oldham police court with stealing a lever watch worth £7 from Joseph Lees, a member of the Oldham team. Lees said he spoke to the prisoner in the Red Lion at half past 11 on Saturday night. His watch was subsequently found in her possession. Miss Shaw was discharged promising to amend.

Swinton with the Challenge Cup in 1900. The players are, back row: G. Jones. Third row (left to right): Jack Evans, Preston, Vigors, Pollitt, B. Murphy. Second row: Tickle, Hampson, R. Valentine, Jim Valentine, Messer, Lewis, Chorley, Harris. Front row: Morgan, Dai Davies.

The final was originally planned to be held at Headingley, Leeds. However, it was thought that the contest between the great Manchester rivals of Salford and Swinton should take place at the Fallowfield Stadium.

The official attendance was 17,864, but thousands more witnessed the game when gates were broken down. Salford were the first to score when their forwards dribbled and hacked the ball almost the length of the field and from a scrum, Griffiths passed to Williams who beat the Lions defence to score a try which Griffiths converted. Within two minutes Swinton equalised when quick passing between their backs scattered the Salford defence, and Bob Messer raced over for a great try which Jim Valentine converted. The game continued at a fast pace with the Salford forwards bustling tactics giving the Reds a firm grip on the game, and shortly before half-time the Salford six dribbled the ball down the field until Arthur Pearson scored when he dropped on the ball over the line.

The Lions responded immediately when 'Lewis scored a try following an excellent passing movement from a scrum on the Salford 25.' In the final minutes of the first half, Salford forward Bill Brown was sent-off for kicking, and Jim Valentine retired with a shoulder injury. In the second half Swinton's backs were superb. The *Manchester Guardian* commented, 'the Swinton halves played with excellent judgement throughout and the three-quarters gave one of the best displays I have seen this season.' Bob Valentine added a try, then calmly walked back to hand the ball to his brother Jim who converted, and later Lewis added the final try to give Swinton a 16-8 victory.

A rare copy of the earliest known example of a Challenge Cup Final programme.

An illustration from the front page of the *Athletic News* depicting the Swinton Lion's roar following the Challenge Cup victory.

An incident during the 1901 Batley v Warrington Challenge Cup Final. The photograph shows a group of Batley players tending to an injured colleague and captures part of the vast crowd of 29,569 that had packed into the Headingley ground, and a few brave supporters who had scaled the main stand roof for a better view. It was estimated that the attendance was over 30,000, with several officials and their guests entering the ground without passing through turnstiles. Many of the supporters in the crowd had travelled from Warrington on six excursion trains, each of which hauled 64 saloon cars.

Batley's Wattie Davies about to take a kick at goal during the 1901 final. The game was unusual in that neither side kicked a goal.

A scrum during the 1901 final.

The Warrington team race from their line in 1901.

Batley team and officials, 1901.

Back row (left to right): Mr William Cairns (assistant trainer), Mr Joe Wilson (trainer), Mr Mark Shackleton (trainer). Second back row: Frank Hollingworth, 'Bob' Spurr, Dai Fitzgerald, Ike Carroll, Pat Judge, Jim Midgley. Second front row: Fred 'Ted' Fozzard, George Main, Jack Rogers, Joe Oakland (captain), Frederic Wilfrid Hoyle, 'Wilf' Auty, Richard Lloyd, Joe Wolstenholme. Front row: Charlie Stubley, 'Wattie' Davies, Arthur Garner, John B. Goodall.

In the days leading up to the final many thought that the clever style of football which the Warrington backs played would be enough to defeat Batley. However, the Gallant Youths were a very experienced team, and masters in the tactics that were necessary to win the intensity of sudden death cup ties. The *Bradford Daily Telegraph* commented on their methods: 'Batley are equally good at seizing an opening or at covering up a mistake. Their success lies less in what they gain than in what they prevent the other side from gaining. Mistakes against Batley are generally fatal.' The Batley forwards had full control of the game and never gave the Warrington backs the chance to get their passing movements flowing. In the first half Goodall pounced on a mistake by Dickenson, dribbled to the Warrington '25' and then picked up and passed to Davies, who 'galloped' over for a try. Minutes later clever passing between Oakland, Midgley and Fitzgerald created an opening for Wilf Auty to score. The second half developed into a dull, monotonous series of scrums and pointless kicking and, at times, bouts of rough play. Shortly before full time, Batley's George Main was sent-off for violence in a tackle. The final whistle eventually blew, and the Gallant Youths had won their third Challenge Cup in five years.

Broughton Rangers. 1902. Players only, back row (left to right): Thompson, Trotter, Winskill. Third row: Widdowson, Stead, Ruddick, S. James, Fielding, Harry. Seated: Garrity, Hogg, Wilson, Whitehead, Oram. Front row: W. James and Barrett.

Some of the players are wearing their Lancashire County shirts rather than the traditional navy blue and white hoops of Broughton.

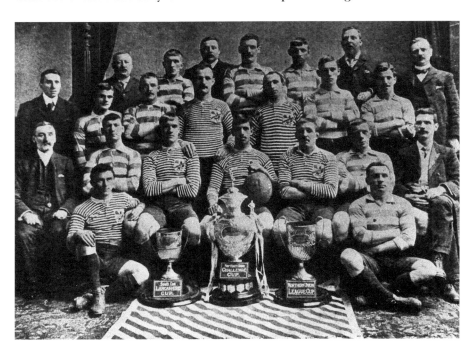

The final between the Manchester rivals of Salford and Broughton Rangers was held at the Athletic Grounds, the home of Rochdale Hornets – a somewhat strange decision, as previously all Lancashire finals had been held at Fallowfield. A poor crowd of 15,000 packed the three parts of the ground that were open; the railway side stand was closed having been deemed unsafe. Salford arrived late; their train had been caught up in a bottleneck on the lines leading to Rochdale. When the game eventually started, a 'boisterous' wind was blowing across the ground. Salford started well and attacked the Rangers line for the first ten minutes. Broughton then gained the advantage, when Sam James collected the ball from a scrum in midfield and transferred to Frank Harry who immediately passed to Bob Wilson. The *Leeds Mercury* described Wilson's progress: 'the Broughton captain, with Hogg in close attendance, galloped away, and with a dummy pass, doubled inside dodged Smith, and ran in between the posts.' Willie James converted. It was the first of three superb tries Bob Wilson scored that April afternoon. In the second half, with Broughton holding a 15-point lead, Salford simply fell to pieces, the *Yorkshire Post* commenting, 'their bungling was really pitiful to watch. Many of their passing movements were spoiled and utilised by the Rangers, who were smart at intercepting transfers.' Broughton had almost complete control and added a further ten points to their lead to give them a 25-0 victory, at the time the most decisive in the history of the final of the competition.

Robert 'Bob' Wilson, the Broughton Rangers captain and the first man to score a hat-trick of tries in a Challenge Cup Final. Wilson was born in Carnforth, where he played his early football for the town's club. He then moved to Morecambe and, when spotted by scouts, 'went south' to sign for Broughton Rangers for the 1900/01 season. Wilson excelled with the South Manchester-based Broughton and he was promoted to captain for the 1901/02 season, when Broughton were League Champions and Challenge Cup winners.

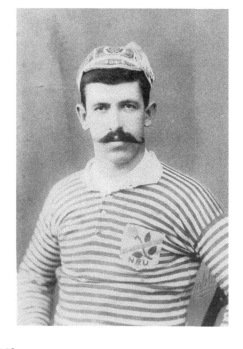

An illustration from the *Athletic News* depicting the 1903 Challenge Cup Final. The Halifax v Salford game attracted a huge crowd of 32,507, a new record for a Northern Union match. The Headingley terraces were so packed that early in the first half barriers gave way and a small section of the crowd burst on to the pitch. The incident was soon contained when most of the supporters went back onto the terraces,

and several more sat on the grass at the side of the pitch. The contest was a poor one, dominated by dull forward play. It was reported that 'in the first few minutes it was obvious that no very finished or artistic football was going to be witnessed.' The Halifax forwards started in a determined mood, and the *Manchester Guardian* described their methods thus: 'every now and then the blue and white forwards would come through the scrummage with the ball at their feet, sweep the scarlet Salfordians aside, and dash up the field in movements which gathered violence like a mountain torrent.' The Salford forwards began to pack the scrums in a very loose fashion to help them break fast to try and stop the Halifax men, so much so that referee Bruckshaw of Stockport paused the game to lecture both sets of forwards on the art of correct and lawful scrum methods. With the game locked at 0-0 at half-time, the Yorkshiremen broke the deadlock early in the second half when Bartle scored a try which Hadwen converted. Later Hadwen kicked a penalty to give Halifax a 7-0 victory in a hugely disappointing final. The Halifax team and officials returned home on a train decorated with the club colours and on arrival in Halifax the team and the cup boarded a charabanc to take them to a reception at the town hall. However, the vehicle pulled up after a few yards and on inspection it was found that one of the axles was badly damaged and a wheel was in danger of falling off. The party disembarked and the cup transferred to the Lord Mayor's carriage. The players then walked to the town hall reception whilst the cup was paraded around the town.

An illustration from the *Athletic News* featuring the 1904 Swinton v Warrington first-round tie. The game was a drab 0-0 draw, with both sides playing well below their best form. Warrington won the replay 20-0 at Wilderspool.

The Halifax v Hunslet 1904 semi-final depicted on the front page of the *Athletic News*. A huge crowd of 21,000 attended the game and the Doncaster Road, out of the city centre towards Wakefield Trinity's Belle Vue ground, was said to be 'packed with charabancs, trams and horse-drawn vehicles.' It was thought that the Northern Union committee had made a mistake in awarding Wakefield the semi-final tie, arguing that the compact ground would struggle with a crowd above 10,000. The *Athletic News*

commented that the game should have been played at Fartown: 'where there is an arena of magnificent arrangement, and a terrace which always commands admiration and gives the occupants the finest possible sight of the field.' With the vast crowd safely in place, the game kicked-off on time, and it was obvious from the start that both sides would be using their forwards to attempt a victory. The Halifax pack constantly packed loose, wheeled and broke fast to set up dribbling rushes whilst the Hunslet eight preferred to heel the ball to their captain Albert Goldthorpe, expecting him to decide the mode of play. Albert gave the Hunslet backs great possession of the ball, but they made nothing of the opportunities, the *Leeds Mercury* recording the Parksiders play as a 'miserable exhibition of three-quarter back play, a deplorable display of inability to finish movements.' The Halifax defence was superb; their spotting and deadly tackling stopped the

majority of Hunslet attacks before they became dangerous. They also kept a close watch on the clever goal-kicking Goldthorpe brothers, tackling them to distraction. The Halifax tactics worked well and gave them a 7-2 victory and a place in their second final.

The *Athletic News* published this illustration featuring Halifax v Warrington Challenge Cup Final on the front page of the issue for 2 May 1904. Halifax defeated Warrington 8-3 to become the second club to win the trophy in consecutive seasons, and the first to win a final outside their own county. The final at Weaste, Salford, attracted a poor crowd of 17,041. The game lacked great skill but was never boring, the *Manchester Guardian* commenting, 'the great achievement of the two sides was that, while they failed to play brilliant football, they never for a moment failed to interest the people who were watching them.' Halifax adopted the methods that had got them to the final, and the *Yorkshire Post* described their methods: 'Halifax won largely by the method in which the forwards broke up the scrums, wheeled the ball onto the Warrington backs, and thereby smashed up the latter's scoring combinations.' Halifax gained the advantage in the first half when Nettleton collected the ball from a scrum and quickly passed to Morley, who gave to Joe Riley who sped past Isherwood to score under the posts. Herbert Hadwen converted the try.

In the second half the Warrington forwards improved and set their backs in motion. The ball was worked across the three-quarters to Jack Fish, who raced down the touchline until faced with the Halifax cover defence racing across the field to stop him. The experienced Fish launched a clever kick over their heads for Davies, who had followed the attack, to gather the ball and speed past full-back Billy Little to score in the corner. Jack Fish failed with the conversion but, encouraged by the score, Warrington became a different team and launched themselves at the Halifax defence. However, Warrington lacked the resolve of the cup holders and, following a strong forward rush, half-back Johnny Morley, the Halifax captain, burst through a breaking scrum and scored a superb individual try to give Halifax a 8-3 win and their second cup final success.

Warrington with the Challenge Cup in 1905.

Back row (left to right): Hackett (trainer), Harmer, Shugars, Preston, Boardman, Belton, Jolley, Heeson (trainer). Seated: Swift, Kenton, Dickenson, Hallam, Isherwood, Fish, Jenkins. Front row: Thomas, Davies, Brooks, Naylor.

A dull and damp day in Leeds reduced the attendance for the Hull Kingston Rovers v Warrington final tie at Headingley to 19,638. The intermittent showers that had fallen in the morning had softened the Headingley pitch, and the turf soon cut up but was still firm enough for some good play. The heavy pitch gave the weightier Rover's forwards a slight advantage; however, the Hull backs could not pierce the Warrington defence, and at half-time the game was locked at 0-0. Three minutes into the second half, Warrington's Jack Fish scored a slightly dubious try when he grounded the ball when seemingly held firm in a tackle. However,

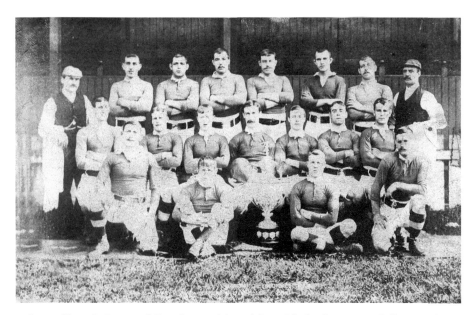

referee Bruckshaw of Stockport blew his whistle for a try. Minutes later Warrington's Ernie Brooks collected the ball from a scrum and sprinted away with Fish in close attendance. The *Athletic News* recorded perfectly a moment of classic Northern Union Football play: 'every eye was watching the movement. Would Brooks pass too soon or too late? Fish was keeping just nicely behind the half-back and about two yards distance. The critical moment came; Sinclair, the Rovers full-back, was bound to go for the man with the ball. He made his spring, and at the precise second the ball flew to Fish and he flew to the line.' It was the last score of the game and Warrington were worthy winners of their first Challenge Cup.

Action from the 1906 Batley v Bradford semi-final. A crowd of 15,707 witnessed a good entertaining game at Fartown. The teams adopted contrasting methods of play dictated by their captains; Bradford's George Marsden, confident in his backs' abilities, constantly opened play out to the three-quarters. However, Batley captain

Joe Oakland favoured his forwards and did his best to close the game down with persistent touch-kicking. The Bradfordians' methods were successful and they were 11-3 winners.

1906 caricatures of the prominent players involved in the Challenge Cup Final. These predominantly unassuming working-class young men had attained celebrity status in their local communities thanks to their ability on the football field.

Bradford with the Challenge Cup in 1906. There are no known surviving records of the identities of the players. The tenth Northern Union Challenge Cup Final generated a great deal of interest on both sides of the Pennines, and the game at Headingley was expected to create a new attendance record. Unfortunately, the notorious Yorkshire weather intervened, and rain and sleet showers were driven across Leeds by a wind that at times reached gale force and reduced the crowd to 15,834 hardy fans who braved the elements. The weather played its part in dictating tactics and the game soon developed into a dull display of endless scrums, with Salford simply launching huge kicks into the Bradford half following up and hoping for a mistake. Bradford, playing into a fierce wind and occasional bouts of sleet and snow, kept the ball moving with short passing movements between the forwards. The first 40 minutes continued in this monotonous way and the teams changed ends with the score at 0-0. In the second half play opened a little, with the Bradford half-backs Marsden and Brear controlling the game, the *Athletic News*

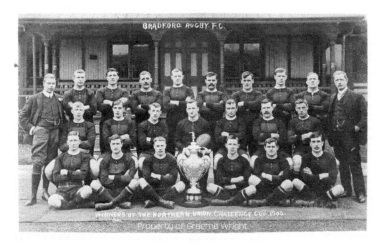

commenting, 'Marsden is a player of resource and smartness, he was well partnered by Brear, a clever half-back. Between them they kept the Salford attack from developing too easily, they put in an enormous amount of tackling.' It was Brear who opened the scoring for Bradford when, with 15 minutes remaining, he burst over the line from a scrum close to the Salford line. Marsden missed the goal attempt, but later Alex Laidlaw kicked a superb penalty. In the final minutes Bradford's Harry Feather and Silas Warwick of Warrington were sent off for fighting and the game ended with a 5-0 victory for Bradford. Following the presentation of the cup, the Bradford party, with a break from traditional rail travel, were driven home in a fleet of vehicles. A small crowd depleted by the weather were waiting in Town Hall Square to witness the cavalcade of around 20 charabancs, waggonettes and smaller vehicles pass through on to the club headquarters at the Alexandra Hotel, where a brief stop was made, before the team travelled to the Osborne Hotel for a 'substantial' tea. The players then visited older Bradford players who were publicans, Tom Broadley at the Punch Bowl, Jack Toothill at the Gardener's Arms and F. W. Cooper at the Palace Hotel. The party then moved on to the Empire Theatre where the cup, accompanied by George Marsden and Sam Brear, was displayed on the illuminated stage.

Warrington with the Challenge Cup at their Wilderspool ground in 1907. Back row (left to right): Hackett (trainer), Shugars, Boardman, Belton, Heath, Harmer, Heeson (assistant trainer). Seated: Brooks, Taylor, Isherwood, Fish, Tilley, Jordon. On ground: Naylor, Hockenhall, Lees, Thomas.

There had been a great deal of speculation in the southern-based press, and in certain northern newspapers, that the Northern Union was dying a natural death. However, the scenes outside Wheater's Field, Broughton, for the 1907 Challenge Cup Final contradicted these views as the *Manchester Courier* eye-witness account recorded, 'both clubs were strongly supported by a large body of wholehearted followers, who were not content with wearing the club colours in their hats and coats but carried in their hands the old time police rattles and other instruments to create a noise, the result was that from long before the players reached the ground the vicinity was a regular pandemonium.' The price of admission had been doubled, but the charge of one shilling did not deter the Northern Union enthusiasts from witnessing the game. And 18,500, including two excursion trains of fans from the West Riding of Yorkshire, packed into the ground. The final was the first to be played by 13-a-side teams, but as an advertisement for the new rules, the game was a failure, with both sides adopting the old-fashioned kick-and-rush methods. Shortly before half-time Oldham produced a fine moment of football when Arthur Lees dodged through and passed to Bert Avery, who scored an unconverted try. Later Jack Fish kicked a penalty. Warrington took the lead in the second half when Sam Lees crossed for a try, which Fish converted. Warrington's captain Jack Fish had a quiet game, but with just eight minutes remaining, the experienced Fish struck when he pounced on a loose ball and delighted the Warrington supporters with a superb piece of opportunist play, which the *Leeds Mercury* described as follows: 'dribbling along he kept the ball under perfect control until past the centre line, when it bounced exactly the right height for him, and, gathering beautifully with one arm, he swerved inside past Thomas, the Oldham full-back, and finished a great movement by scoring between the posts and then kicking a goal.' Minutes later Tom Hockenhall dribbled the ball past the Oldham defence and scored a try which Jack Fish converted to give Warrington a 17-3 victory.

Jack Fish was one of the many talented players in the Northern Union. Jack was the idol of the Warrington followers and many would fashion lengths of wire into the shape of a fish and wave them at matches. He signed for Warrington in 1898 from junior club Lostock Gralam and stayed at the club until his retirement in 1911. Jack made 321 appearances, scoring 215 tries and 262 goals, represented England three times and won 16 caps for Lancashire. Jack was an exceptional sprinter and took part in many professional races.

The *Athletic News* illustration for the 1907 Challenge Cup Final captures a Warrington supporter holding aloft a wire fish.

Hunslet v Oldham Challenge Cup second round, 1908. The two clubs were neck and neck at the top of the league Championship table and the Parksiders were enjoying their finest-ever season. The south Leeds-based club had recruited well and had built a superb pack of forwards, and a clever set of backs. Led by their inspirational captain Albert Goldthorpe, Hunslet were a major force in the Northern Union. The cup tie generated tremendous interest and Hunslet had 100 posters printed and displayed around south Leeds. A huge crowd of 20,000 packed into Parkside. For the first time that season Hunslet were without Albert Goldthorpe, and with his understudy Fred Whittaker out of action with influenza, the selection committee took a gamble and played forward Bill Jukes at half-back. The gamble worked well as Jukes had a superb game and a hand in two of the Hunslet tries. It was the stamina of the Terrible Six that laid the foundations for a 15-8 victory, with tries from Fred Farrar (2), Harry Wilson and two goals from Walter Goldthorpe and a drop from Billy Eagers. The *Oldham Evening Chronicle* commented: 'the Hunslet forwards were not really any better than the Oldham six. Yet by their dare-devil tactics they beat the Oldham forwards continually, beat them for possession, in the scrummages, and beat them in the open.' Oldham's points came from tries from Avery and Llewellyn and a goal from Ferguson.

Football Crowd, Barrow v. Hunslet.
MARCH 28TH. 1908

A section of the record crowd of 12,000 for the Barrow v Hunslet third-round Challenge Cup match at Cavendish Park on 28 March 1908. The Hunslet party had stayed overnight at Furness Abbey to avoid the long journey. The Parksiders were in top form, defeating Barrow 8-0. Batten and Smales scored tries and Albert Goldthorpe dropped a goal.

The usual *Athletic News* illustration featuring scenes from the 1908 Challenge Cup semi-final at Central Park, Wigan. Hunslet arrived early in Wigan, and at their temporary base in the town the players enjoyed a couple of hours' sleep. The peace and quiet calmed the players' nerves and revitalised them for the important game ahead of them. Broughton Rangers were favourites to win – their superb backs, led by Bob Wilson, were expected to outclass Hunslet. However, the Terrible Six played their finest game of the season,  'Forward' of the *Leeds Mercury* commenting, 'it must have been a revelation to Bob Wilson to see his fellow backs hopelessly at a loss to make any headway against the robust attention paid them by the Parkside forwards. Harry Wilson and co excelled themselves. In the art of securing possession, they were masters, and not wasted in the loose.' Behind these powerful forwards was Albert Goldthorpe the master schemer. The *Athletic News* commented, 'Albert Goldthorpe – surely the greatest leader of present-day teams – gave so many illustrations of how to play the touch game. The Hunslet captain played the ball low, rushed round the scrummage, and then; a neat punt between the Broughton scrum half and the three-quarter, and the ball rolled into touch, with 20 or 30 yards gained.' The Parksiders routed the Rangers 16-2 with tries from Farrar, Batten, Smith (2) and two goals from Albert Goldthorpe, one a drop from the touch line with his left foot. Barlow kicked a goal for Broughton.

Hunslet with the Challenge Cup in 1908. The players are, back row (left to right): J. T. Wray, W. Goldthorpe, Smales, W. Hannah (trainer), C. Cappleman, Randall, W. Jukes. Middle row: W. Wray, C. Ward, W. Ward, A. Goldthorpe, Batten, H. Place, W. Brookes, J. Wilson. Front row: W. Hoyle, F. Whittaker, F. Smith, W. Eagers. Hunslet were the first club to win All Four Cups available. The Challenge Cup Final was played for the first time at Fartown. Heavy snow showers had fallen during the morning and had made the pitch heavy going. Despite the weather, supporters of both clubs poured into the town. The LNER ran seven special trains from Hull.

It was the weather that once again dictated the tactics in a Challenge Cup Final. The *Leeds Mercury* commented, 'the state of the ground was largely responsible for a good many blunders, and for a preponderance of kicking over running and passing, Hunslet recovered better from their blunders than Hull and they kicked with better judgement.' Hull started the game in a determined way, but their movements were checked either by the Hunslet defence or the atrocious state of the Fartown turf. The Parkside forwards gradually began to gain most of the possession from the scrums.

HUNSLET C.F&A. CLUB. 1907·8.

20 minutes into the game and from a scrum Fred Smith passed to Walter Goldthorpe, who quickly transferred to Billy Eagers. The unpredictable Eagers fooled the Hull defence when, as the *Athletic News* described, 'Hull expected Eagers to mechanically pass to Farrar; but on the contrary he wheeled round and with his left foot kicked a goal.' Five minutes before half-time Albert Goldthorpe passed to his half-back partner Fred Smith, who beat the Hull defence for a try which Albert converted to give the Parksiders a 7-0 lead. The second half was played in a fierce snowstorm, the *Athletic News* commenting, 'miserable it was for the 18,000 onlookers, and miserable it was for the players who, in the swirling, blinding snow, were expected to field and pass and kick as though the pitch were fast, the air of the balminess we expect at the approach of May, and the ball firm and dry.' The players braved the conditions and Albert Goldthorpe kicked a goal from a mark and, with minutes remaining, Eagers passed to Farrar

who scored a try, which Albert Goldthorpe converted to give Hunslet a 14-0 victory.

A rare score card from the 1908 final.

The Hunslet and Leeds players pictured together prior to the second-round Challenge Cup match at Parkside in March 1909. There is no surviving record of the players' names, However, some of the players are known; standing far left is Frank 'Bucket' Young, the Leeds full-back. Seated on the front row in the dark shirts are, left to right, Hunslet players Billy Jukes, Fred Smith, Billy Batten, Bill Brookes and, on the far-right standing, Billy Hannah, the Hunslet trainer. Interest in derby games between Leeds rivals was always high, and with the added attraction of a Challenge Cup tie, a huge crowd of 22,000 packed into Parkside. Hunslet defeated Leeds 15-9, with tries from Farrar, Walsh and Eagers, Cappleman kicked two goals and Albert Goldthorpe dropped one. For Leeds, Desborough scored a try and Frank Young kicked three goals. The Parksiders' Terrible Six were on top form and 'keen and energetic' from start to finish.

Wakefield Trinity defeated Wigan in the 1909 Challenge Cup semi-final at Wheater's Field, Broughton. The Trinitarians were always the masters of the game; the *Yorkshire Post* commenting, 'Wakefield possessed the dash and directness which pay best in a stern cup-tie. The stamina and scrummaging power of their forwards were the factors which gave the victors their commanding position.' Newbould and Metcalfe were superb, their clever tactical play supplementing the forwards. A crowd of 18,000 witnessed Trinity defeat Wigan 14-2, with Newbould and Bennett scoring tries and Metcalfe (3) and Holmes kicking goals. Leytham scored Wigan's points with a goal.

The *Athletic News* illustration for the 1909 Wakefield Trinity v Hull FC final at Headingley. Once again, a Challenge Cup Final at Headingley attracted huge crowds and an official attendance of 23,587 was recorded, but 30 minutes before the kick-off the huge crowds at the Bowling Green

entrances caused the gates to give way, and thousands surged into the ground without paying. The attendance was later estimated to be almost 30,000. Once again, the weather played its part in a Challenge Cup Final. Heavy rain had fallen throughout the night and during the morning, making the Headingley pitch soft and treacherous underfoot. The conditions dismissed any thoughts of open, attractive football. The state of the turf favoured old-fashioned forward play and Trinity excelled. It was reported that six of the Wakefield 13 had worked during the week on the night shift and consequently missed the special training sessions. On the day of the final the Trinitarians were superb, the *Athletic News* commenting: 'the Hull players were thoroughly outmanoeuvred and overplayed. Their forwards were swept aside with ease and the backs were denied any opportunities.' Wakefield opened the scoring early in the game when Tommy Newbould collected the ball from a scrum, outwitted the Hull half-backs and burst through three Hull forwards for a try, and later Bennett scored to give Trinity a 6-0 lead at half-time. In the second half Wakefield were in almost complete control and Crosland, Simpson and Bennett scored tries and Metcalfe kicked a goal to give them a 17-0 victory. The *Manchester Guardian* commented, 'as an exhibition of skill, intelligence and pluck, Wakefield's success deserves a flattering place in Northern Union history.'

Following the presentation of the cup, the Wakefield players and committee members boarded a special illuminated electric tram provided by the Wakefield and District Light Railway Company. The tram was decorated with 400 red-and-blue lights and many banners. The tram left Headingley at 6pm and made its way to Wakefield and was met by a brass band at Lofthouse and then continued into the city centre, where a dense crowd had gathered near the cathedral. The tram made its way to Trinity's headquarters at the Alexander Hotel in Belle Vue, where the team had dinner, had their medals presented by the mayor of Wakefield, and enjoyed several toasts. The players and the cup then made a tour of several of the city's pubs to greet their supporters.

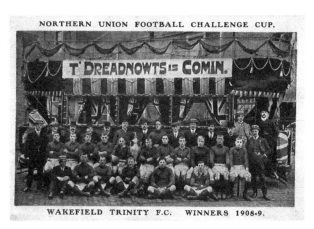

NORTHERN UNION FOOTBALL CHALLENGE CUP.

T' DREADNOWTS IS COMIN.

WAKEFIELD TRINITY F.C.   WINNERS 1908-9.

James D. Metcalfe (Jimmy) with the Challenge Cup in 1909. Born in Cockermouth, Cumberland, in 1873, Jimmy played his early football for Askam Rugby Union, and then in 1890 he moved to South Yorkshire to play for Barnsley Rugby Union Club. After seven years with the Barnsley club, he joined Featherstone Rugby Union Club. Jimmy left Featherstone to join Wakefield Trinity NU club and made his debut in September 1897. Metcalfe became a superb full-back and deadly goal kicker at Wakefield. His solid defensive work and outstanding kicking led to Yorkshire County honours during the 1897/98 and 1898/99 seasons. James Metcalfe made 374 appearances for Wakefield, scoring three tries and kicking 386 goals, a total of 781 points. He retired during the 1910/11 season.

Wakefield Trinity with the Challenge Cup in 1909. Back row (left to right): J. Taylor, Bennett, W. Lynch, P. Unsworth, Mr J. B. Cooke, A. Crosland, H. Beaumont, J. Walton, G. Taylor. Middle row: Mr E. Parker, H. Kershaw, J. D. Metcalfe, H. Slater, J. Auton, S. Parkes. Front row: D. Holmes, W. G. Simpson, T. H. Newbould, E. Sidwell.

The scenes outside Fartown on Saturday, 16 April, the afternoon of the 1910 Challenge Cup Final. Torrential rain began to fall in Huddersfield around noon. The weather was not the only problem on the day of the final; the usually smooth railway arrangements broke down and with all the football enthusiasts travelling from the east of Huddersfield, a huge blockage on the rail lines between Leeds and Huddersfield brought  trains to a halt. Both teams were caught in the jam and eventually contacted the officials at Fartown. Various messengers were relayed to Huddersfield giving conflicting estimated times of arrival. A vast crowd, estimated at 20,000, waited patiently for the game to commence and eventually the teams arrived, and the game kicked off at 4.20pm, almost an hour late. Leeds started the game well and two minutes from kick-off Frank 'Bucket' Young, their Welsh full-back, kicked a penalty. Then 15 minutes later the Loiners' half-back Jimmy Sanders was injured and had to leave the field and took no further part in the game. Hull soon took advantage of their extra man; Cottrell scored a try and Rogers and Wallace kicked goals to give Hull a 7-2 half-time advantage. Leeds played exceptionally well in the second half. The *Athletic News* commented, 'the Leeds forwards had ideas which could hardly be described as original, but, their fiery tackling, their desperate earnestness, and above all, their wonderful staying powers entitle them most credit in a game that can only be remembered for the strenuous character of the play.' Walter Goldthorpe scored a try and Frank Young kicked a penalty to create the first-ever draw in a Challenge Cup Final. At the final whistle the Leeds players were loath to leave the field, sensing a victory should extra time be played. The NU committee members hastily held a meeting and decided against extra time and instead, realising that some of the players were due to depart for the Lions' tour, arranged for a reply to be played on Monday, 18 April at Fartown, with extra time to be played should the game be a draw at full time.

Mrs Houghton, the wife of the president of the NU, sits with the Challenge Cup during the 1910 replay at Fartown. Mrs Houghton had travelled from Southport to present the cup due to her husband, Mr J. H. Houghton, being away en route to Australia with the tourists. A good crowd of 11,608 attended the replay. Leeds were fortunate to win the toss for choice of ends and gained the benefit of a strong wind behind them. They soon opened the scoring with a penalty goal from Frank Young and, 15 minutes later, the Welsh full-back dropped a superb goal. Leeds gradually took control and tries from Webster, and Topham and three goals from Young gave the

Loiners a 16-0 lead at half-time. In the second half veteran Walter Goldthorpe took advantage of a Hull mistake and scored a try, and two minutes later Harold Rowe sprinted through a weak Hull defence to cross for a try under the posts. Frank Young converted both tries to give the Loiners a 26-0 lead. The Airlie Birds finally responded and a penalty from Ned Rogers, with tries from Walton and Connell and two conversions, made the final score 26-12. The game ended in confusion when the referee and a linesman were attacked by two spectators who had invaded the pitch. The police, aided by Leeds forward Harry Topham, soon controlled the situation.

Leeds with the 1910 Challenge Cup. Back row (left to right): Morn (trainer), Goldthorpe, Barron, Topham, W. Ward, Biggs. Middle row: Sanders, Ware, Webster, Harrison, Whitaker, Rowe. Front row: Fawcett, Young, Gillie, Jarman.

A section of the 18,000-crowd at the Willows, Salford, for the 1911 Broughton Rangers v Rochdale Hornets Challenge Cup semi-final. The Rangers overcame the strong challenge from the Hornets forwards to win 12-9.

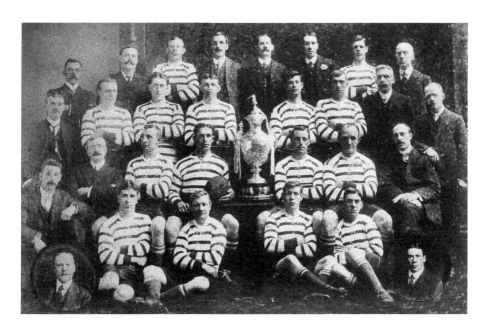

Broughton Rangers cup winners, 1911. Players only, back row (left to right): Heys, Bouch. Third row: Hirst, Gorry, Winskill, R. Clampitt, Robinson. Seated: Wild, J. Clampitt, Harris, Ruddick. Front row: Davidson, Jones, Barlow, Scott. The 1911 final was played at Salford, where heavy rain had fallen on Friday night and Saturday morning – the Willows pitch was a quagmire with pools of water covering parts of the playing surface. On their arrival in Salford, officials of the Wigan club immediately called for the game to be postponed. The Northern Union committee members present made a close inspection of the pitch and declared it fit to play on. It was thought at the time that the number of spectators in the ground at the time of the inspection greatly influenced the decision to play the game. The game kicked-off and for a few minutes players were able to keep their feet and handle the ball, but soon the turf cut up and the field became a bog. The Wigan forwards did well and gained most of the possession from the scrums. However, when the Wigan half-backs threw the ball to the backs, they often would drop the ball. Eventually some of the most talented backs in the Northern Union were reduced to a group of muddied oafs who could only slip, slide and tumble their way around the pitch. The Broughton forwards soon adapted to the conditions, and the *Leeds Mercury* described the six thus: 'The Rangers forwards were strong and quick and wheeled and broke up the scrums rapidly.' The Rangers forwards then simply swept through the Wigan team. Broughton's clever use of the correct methods for the conditions were successful and they defeated Wigan 4-0 thanks to two penalty goals from Billy Harris. Many people thought that Broughton only won because of the conditions, although others believed that if the Rangers could beat Wigan in mud, they would trounce them in firm and dry conditions.

Dewsbury with the Challenge Cup at their Crown Flatt ground in 1912. Players only, back row (left to right): Abbishaw, Barnett, O'Neill, Hamill. Middle row: Evans, Ward, Rhodes, Richardson, Sharples, Ware, Jackett. Front row: Milner and Neary. The final, held at Headingley, attracted a poor crowd of 16,000. Large numbers of Oldham supporters thought the final was a guaranteed victory for their team, the majority deciding not to travel to Leeds, as Oldham were firm favourites to defeat Dewsbury. However, the Yorkshire 13 played with grit and determination that astonished their critics and delighted the mainly Yorkshire crowd, the *Yorkshire Post* commenting, 'The Dewsbury forwards were the quicker and stronger set, the half-backs, Milner and Neary, passed out very smartly indeed and the team were not afraid of tackling Oldham by means of the open game. There was none of the kick-and-rush business about their method of play and if there had been a little more polish in the attack Oldham could have been beaten quite easily.' Oldham opened the scoring when Joe Ferguson kicked a penalty goal. Five minutes later Dewsbury equalised when described by the *Yorkshire Post*: 'There was a scrummage in front of the Oldham goal, the ball came out to Milner, who flashed it across to Neary, and that player immediately kicked over the bar. It was all done in a couple of seconds and

before the scrum had broken up.' 20 minutes later James Lomas charged down the field, fooled the approaching defenders and set in motion a bout of passing which led to George Cook scoring a try. Then 20 minutes into the second half Dewsbury lost the services of Joe Hammill, their strong running forward, with a bad knee injury. Ten minutes later the teams were numerically even when, following a scuffle at a scrum, Bert Avery, the Oldham forward, voiced an opinion regarding referee Ennion's ability and was immediately sent-off for impertinence. The Northern Union had a strict code of practice regarding players' behaviour, which referees followed enthusiastically. Little was said in defence of Avery's punishment. With around eight minutes play remaining, and Oldham holding on to a three-point lead, Oldham's Australian half-back Arthur Anlezark made a careless kick from a scrum, which Dewsbury wingman Rhodes caught and swept over the line unopposed for an unconverted try that levelled the score. Sensing a famous victory, the Dewsbury players swarmed towards the Oldham line and from a scrum Tommy Milner quickly hurled the ball to Billy Rhodes, who managed to touch the ball down over the line and inches from touch. Unsure about the try, referee Ennion consulted his linesman, Mr H. Schofield, who immediately gave the try. Ware missed the difficult conversion, but it mattered little for two minutes later the whistle blew for full time and Dewsbury were 8-5 winners. On their return to Dewsbury the players and officials were given the sad news that two of their followers

had died during the excitement of the afternoon. Mr Arthur Hirst, the landlord of the Sir Robert Peel Arms, Bradford Road, Dewsbury, and a founder member of the club, and the club treasurer in the early years, suffered a fatal stroke on his way home from Leeds. Mr C. Milner was also taken ill on his return to Dewsbury and died later at home.

Abbishaw and Hamill, two very capable members of the Dewsbury pack. Joe Hamill would later join Hull FC, where he was a member of the team that won the Challenge Cup in 1914.

The Dewsbury captain Fred Richardson with the Challenge Cup at Crown Flatt in 1912. Fred played his early football with Dewsbury Clarence Juniors and Dewsbury Mashers and signed for the club in 1902. He made 303 appearances until his retirement in 1915. His robust style of forward play led to him being given the nickname 'Cosh'.

A section of the crowd at the Boulevard for Hull v Seaton Challenge Cup first-round match in 1913. Hull defeated the junior side from Cumberland 24-2.

Huddersfield with the Challenge Cup in 1913. The players are, back row (left to right): Lee, Clark, Swinden, Wrigley, Longstaff, Higson, Chilcott, Gronow. Middle row: Holland, Davies, Wagstaff, Gleeson, Todd, Moorhouse. Front row: Rosenfeld, Rogers. The Fartowners also won the League Championship and Yorkshire League trophies, which are pictured to the left and right of the Challenge Cup. Huddersfield were firm favourites to defeat Warrington in the final played in the (by now) traditional cup final weather of rain and a fierce wind at Headingley. Receiving the ball from the kick-off, Warrington began the game in a determined fashion, their well-thought out and polished tactics were unassuming but effective. Keen and determined forward play caused them to gain ground with clever and constant tackling. The Warrington half-backs rarely brought their three-quarters into the game, choosing to punt the ball to touch, and trust in the forwards' ability to

wheel the scrums and break quickly to contain the Huddersfield backs. The tactics worked well in the first half, the *Yorkshire Post* commenting, 'over and over again the Huddersfield backs got their passing machinery into motion, yet as each man received the ball, he received a determined tackle also.' In a surprising departure from their habitual adverse comments of Northern Union Football, the *Yorkshire Post* also commented, 'close and impartial followers of Huddersfield's passing and re-passing movements have held the view that the backs are often flattered by the lack of intelligence and want of determination shown by defending sides; hence when the same players were confronted by the deadly Warrington tackling, they hardly knew what to make of it.' Warrington opened the scoring in the 25th minute when from a scrum Nicolas beat Grey and whipped the ball to Bradshaw, who fooled Moorhouse with a dummy and crossed for a try. Full-back Ben Jolley took advantage of the wind and kicked a tremendous conversion from the touch line to give Warrington a well-deserved 5-0 lead. The Warrington players noticeably tired in the second half and were unable to contain the rampant Fartown backs, who, inspired by Harold Wagstaff, created the opportunities for Stanley Moorhouse to become the second player to score a hat-trick of tries in a final, and give Huddersfield a 9-5 victory and their first-ever Challenge Cup trophy.

The team line-ups from the official programme for the 1914 Huddersfield v Hull Challenge Cup semi-final at Headingley. Both clubs had spent vast amounts of money in signing personnel and the players listed are some of the finest in the Northern Union. 30,000 people packed into the ground to witness the game. Huddersfield were the holders of the Challenge Cup and were firm favourites to beat Hull. However, the Hull team were eager to win the Cup and the *Yorkshire Post* commented, 'Whole-hearted endeavour won Hull the match. Their forwards

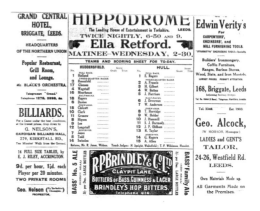

laid the foundation of victory by getting possession of the ball in the scrums.' Each time Huddersfield won the ball, Steve Darmody, Hull's dashing Australian loose forward, quickly broke from the pack to tackle the man with the ball. Half-back Devereaux and centres Batten and Gilbert were also highly effective in defence, their hard-tackling shook and eventually shattered the Fartowners' attack. Hull defeated Huddersfield 11-3 thanks to a try from Holder and four goals from Ned Rogers. Todd scored a try for Huddersfield.

Ned Rogers kicked four goals, one conversion, two penalties and a drop to help Hull defeat Huddersfield in the 1914 semi-final.

Billy Batten fills this sketch of Hull's victory over Wakefield Trinity in the 1914 Challenge Cup Final. The *Athletic News* commented on Batten's performance in the final as follows: 'in the daring raids of Hull in the second half it was Batten who, with the ball tucked under his arm, ploughed through the ranks of the defenders and left beaten opponents in his triumphal course. His courage and determination

without doubt inspired his colleagues to rally round in the closing stages of the game.' Hull's superb victory over Huddersfield in the semi-final made them firm favourites to win the cup and 13 special trains from the city's Paragon Station transported 9,000 of their supporters to Halifax, and an estimated 5,000 travelled from Wakefield to help create a crowd of 19,000 at Thrum Hall. Wakefield kicked off with a slight breeze and the sun behind them and soon had Hull defending. However, the game soon developed into

a dour struggle between the forwards. The Trinitarians created several chances to open the scoring, but their finishing was dreadful. The game continued as a dour scoreless struggle. Five minutes into the second half, Herbert Kershaw, the Trinity captain, was sent off for kicking Alf Francis. The game eventually began to open out and Hull began to use their backs more often, and with eight minutes remaining Billy Anderson collected the ball from a scrum and instantly passed to Devereaux who, with quick thinking, involved Gilbert, who found the ever-eager Batten. He galloped forward, drew the Wakefield defence and launched a perfect pass to Jack Harrison, who crossed in the corner for the first try. With seconds remaining, a clever pass from Bert Gilbert gave Alf Francis the space to score the try to confirm Hull's victory.

Bert Gilbert, the Hull captain, collects the Challenge Cup from Alderman W. H. Ingham, major of Halifax, to become the first Hull captain and first Australian to receive the cup.

The Hull players and officials were anxious to avoid the vast crowds at Halifax station, and soon after the presentation of the cup they boarded a special horse-drawn carriage which was waiting outside Thrum Hall. The carriage took them to Hipperholme station where they boarded a train to take them back to Hull. The train made a stop at Hessle and once again the party boarded a horse-drawn carriage to drive them to the city centre. The players are captured waiting to board their transport.

The party and the cup are ready to travel to the city centre. Bert Gilbert holds the cup and Billy Batten stands on the far right. Thousands welcomed their heroes and it was reported the major streets were packed solid with people hoping to see 'the little stranger' as the cup had been nicknamed by the local papers.

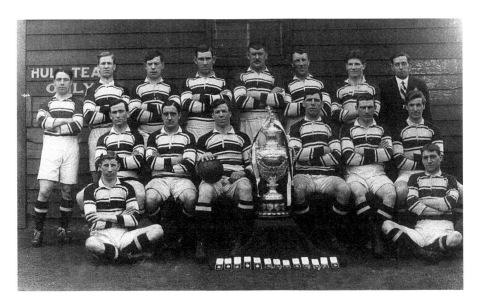

The Hull squad with the Challenge Cup and the players medals at the Boulevard 1914. Back row (left to right): Milner, Darmody, Hammill, Dick Taylor, Herridge, Holder, Oldham, Melville (trainer). Middle row: Devereux, Anderson, Gilbert, Batten, Ned Rogers, Harrison. Front row: Francis and Greg Rogers.

The teams recorded in the official programme for the 1915 Challenge Cup Semi Final held at Parkside. The Semi between Huddersfield and Wigan, arguably the finest clubs in the Union, was expected to produce a classic match and 18,000 football enthusiasts packed into Parkside. The game was not as good as the crowds expected, as Wigan were forced to play a weakened team. Illness kept scrum-half Owen out and Bert Jenkins was left out for disciplinary reasons. This led to some players being out of position. Hayward, a forward, went to centre, and three-quarter Walford played at half-back. Guy, a second-team player, came in at centre. It was thought that the Fartowners' 27-3 victory was due to the weakness and mistakes of the Wigan team rather than their own play. Huddersfield did create some good passing movements, swiftly and accurately developed, but it was more through individual excellence – especially on the part of Rosenfeld – who scored four tries.

At the end of the 1914/15 season Huddersfield matched Hunslet's 1908 achievement of winning all Four Cups – 'the Team of all Talents' with their four cups are pictured at Fartown. Back row (left to right): Lee, Higson, Banks, Jones, Heyes, Longstaff, Clarke, Swinden. Middle row: Habron, Holland, Moorhouse, Wagstaff, Gleeson, Gronow. Front row: Ganley, Rosenfeld, Rogers.

The Fartowners, 'a team of mystery and marvel' won their third trophy in characteristic style, trouncing St Helens 37-3 in the Challenge Cup Final at Oldham. Once again, the British weather played its part in a Challenge Cup Final, with heavy rain drenching Oldham's Watersheddings ground, perched high in the foothills of the Pennines. The heavy rain fell incessantly before and during the game and reduced the attendance to 8,000. St Helens kicked-off with the advantage of the wind and the rain behind them. Within three minutes Tommy Gleeson sprinted forward and beat the Saints defence with a superb side-step to cross for the first try. For the next 20 minutes the St Helens forwards played well and created several chances for their backs. However, it was the incredibly talented Huddersfield backs who took control of the game, and Wagstaff, Rosenfeld, Wagstaff again and Gleeson swept through the Saints' defence for tries to give the Fartowners a 21-point lead at half-time. St Helens' resistance to the Huddersfield onslaught collapsed in the second half, and Holland, Moorhouse, Gronow and Rogers scored tries. The Team of all Talents were a unique force in Northern Union football, taking the game to a higher level of skills and tactics. On that incredibly wet afternoon, high above Oldham the Challenge Cup Trophy, was their third cup of the season, equalling Hunslet's All

Four Cups triumph in 1908. Huddersfield's 37 points were, at the time, the most ever scored in a final. Ben Gronow's five goals brought his total for the season to 140, a new record. The Welsh forward's try that afternoon also helped bring his points scored in a season to 292, another new record. Australian wing man Albert Rosenfeld's solitary try brought his total to 56 for the season, a new record.

John Willie Higson with All Four Cups in 1915. Higson was a member of the Hunslet team that won All Four Cups in 1907/08.

A newspaper sketch depicting incidents during the 1920 first-round Challenge Cup tie between Hull and BOCM FC. The Hull v the Hull-based junior club British Oil and Cake Mills FC created tremendous interest in the city and an incredible crowd of 14,000 packed into the Boulevard to witness the game. As expected, Hull totally overwhelmed the juniors, scoring 17 tries and 12 goals for a 75-2 victory.

Caricatures from the talented Ern Shaw of Hull featuring Hull's 29-10 victory over Batley in the second round of the 1920 Challenge Cup competition.

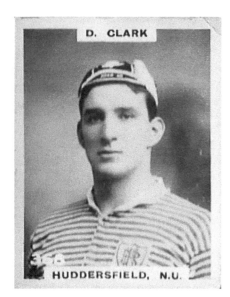

D. CLARK

HUDDERSFIELD, N.U.

Douglas Clark, a try scorer in Huddersfield's 21-10 victory over Wigan in the 1920 Challenge Cup Final. In 1916 Clark joined the Army Service Corps and saw action in France where he was gassed at Passendale. He was later wounded by shrapnel and at the end of hostilities he had a 95 per cent disability certificate. Remarkably, the immensely strong Clark played an important part in Huddersfield's third Challenge Cup Final victory in the 1920 final, the first since World War One curtailed organised competitive NU football in 1915. The final was played at Headingley in persistent and heavy rain. A poor crowd of 14,000 witnessed a well-fought, exciting encounter. Despite the conditions, both sides decided to use their backs and not adopt the kick-and-rush tactics that had been seen in many previous weather-affected finals. Wigan were lucky to take the lead after 20 minutes' play, when Harry Hall kicked over the advancing Huddersfield defence, but when he followed his kick was brought down by Pogson. Referee Mills of Oldham awarded a penalty try, even though Hall still had two Huddersfield men in front of him. Jolley converted and Wigan had a five-point lead. Within ten minutes the Fartowners struck back when a Wagstaff pass put Clark over for a try which Gronow converted. Minutes before half-time Wagstaff put Pogson over for an unconverted try to give Huddersfield an 8-5 half-time lead. Both sides were handling and moving exceptionally well in the inclement conditions and the game was a great spectacle. In the first minutes of the second half Huddersfield were constantly near the Wigan line, but it was Wigan who made the breakthrough when a clever kick from Shaw gave Sid Jerram the edge to beat Pogson to touch down for a try, which Jolley converted with a superb kick from an exceedingly difficult position. Wigan were leading 10-8, but Huddersfield were far from beaten, and with Wigan tiring Harold Wagstaff began to dictate things, the *Leeds Mercury* commenting, 'Wagstaff was a tactician par excellence and he did not waste his passes nor his energy.' In the final 20 minutes the Fartowners' skill and stamina enveloped Wigan and with tries from Habron, Todd and Pogson and two goals from Gronow they swept majestically to their third Challenge Cup Final victory with a 21-10 win.

Huddersfield's Ben Gronow kicked three goals in the 1920 Challenge Cup Final. Born in Bridgend in 1887, the immensely strong Gronow played his early Rugby Union football with the Bridgend senior club and was soon playing for Wales. On 15 January 1910 Ben made Rugby Union history when he kicked-off in the England v Wales match, the first international to be held at Twickenham. He signed for Huddersfield for £120 on 14 May 1910 and went on to play 395 games, kick 673 goals, and score 80 tries for an incredible 1,586 points.

Harold Wagstaff, 'The Prince of Centres' and the first man to captain three Challenge Cup-winning teams.

The programme for the Askam v Bradford Northern Challenge Cup first-round match, 1921. Cumberland-based Askam declined Bradford's request to play the game at their Birch Lane ground and the junior club's confident decision was rewarded with a good attendance at their Duddon Road ground. As expected, the senior side were far too experienced for Askam, whose players, the *Athletic News* commented, 'hugged the ball as though they were playing in a local junior league match.' The home side had a keen defence and their strong tackling held the visitors' backs for most of the game and prevented an embarrassingly high-scoring defeat. In the first half Dobson and Laughlin kicked penalty goals for Bradford and in the second half Surman eventually penetrated the Askam defence and scored an unconverted try. In the final seconds of the game Dixon delighted the home crowd when he kicked a penalty goal to make the score 7-2 to Bradford. The visitors' victory was marred when their second-row forward Halford was sent off in the second half for kicking.

Programme for To-day—26-2-21.

BRADFORD NORTHERN v. ASKAM

AT DUDDON ROAD.

Kick-off 3 p.m.   40 minutes each way.

TEAMS :   ASKAM.

W. BARNES.

T. BURROW.   W. KIRKBY.   T. DIXON.   J. POPE

R. COULSON.   T. WHARTON.

J. PRUTHERER.   J. BOYD.   T. KIRKBY.

J. NANSON.   W. ALEXANDER.   T. FELL.

Referee : Mr. F. FAIRHURST, of Wigan.

MANN.   DOBSON.   HALFORD.

MYERS.   HOLMES.   DOLAN.

MORTIMER.   MELLING.

SMITH.   LAUGHLIN.   SURMAN.   TREHARNE.

OLIVER.

BRADFORD NORTHERN.

TOUCH JUDGES :

Messrs. W. M. Gabbatt (Barrow) & Jas. Atkinson (Dalton)

The Askam Town Prize Band

Will play Selections on the Field from 2 to 3 p.m.

Pages from the official programme published for the 1921 Leigh v Halifax Challenge Cup Final held at The Cliff, Broughton. The final attracted tremendous interest and it was soon apparent the NU had, once again, made a poor choice for the venue of the code's most important event. Half an hour before the kick-off there was little room inside, and an estimated 500 fans broke down two gates to gain admission. It was only the actions of mounted police that stopped the rush and prevented a disaster. Such was the crush that many who had forced their way into the ground soon turned around and left. Many of the crowd

outside turned their attention to a schoolboys' cricket match being played on an adjoining field. The official attendance was eventually estimated to be 25,000.

Halifax were firm favourites to beat Leigh, the *Athletic News* commenting, 'by no stretch of imagination could Leigh be described as Lancashire's leading team.' However, cup finals have famously inspired players to play well above their normal form. From the start Leigh's forwards were the masters of the scrums, the *Athletic News* adding, 'Leigh's great strength was forward, the men played with method, a sensible and correct interpretation of forward possibilities.' With the possession gained, the important battle at half-back went to Leigh. The *Manchester Guardian* recorded, 'Mooney had a splendid partner in Parkinson, and they varied their tactics so frequently that the Halifax backs were always in doubt as to their next line of attack.' Thomas (2) and Parkinson crossed for tries and Clarkson kicked two goals to give the Lancastrians a well-deserved, tactical 13-0 victory.

The Leigh squad and club officials with the 1921 Challenge Cup at Sharples Hall, Bolton.

Rochdale Hornets Challenge Cup winners in 1922. The Hull v Rochdale Challenge Cup Final was the last final to be contested under the Northern Rugby Football Union name and the old title was given a great send-off by the Hull and Rochdale players, who produced a classic – regarded as the finest exhibition of Northern Union football ever seen in a final. The return of the final to the magnificent Headingley Stadium attracted a huge crowd and well before the kick-off the crowd inside the ground was so vast that officials locked the gates with hundreds still outside. Fearing a rush on the gates the officials, following advice from the police, threw the gates open and hundreds poured in. The official attendance was reported to be 34,700, but estimates revised this to 37,000, a new record for a NU match in England. Even the weather favoured the Northern Union and the game kicked off in warm sunshine with a slight breeze. The Headingley turf was reported to be ideal for football and in a superb, firm condition and the game started at a fast pace, during which the Rochdale forwards soon gained control. The *Leeds Mercury* described their play: 'The whole six played together like a well-oiled machine. They heeled well and they wheeled

well, they backed up and tackled and dribbled and altogether gave a display that will make this final memorable.' Hull opened the scoring ten minutes into the game, when Jim Kennedy charged down a poor clearance kick by Heaton and gathered the ball to touch down for an unconverted try. The Hornets soon took the lead when Dick Paddon kicked a brace of penalty goals and then, following a strong forward rush, a superb pass from Louis Corsi created the space for Tommy Fitton to dodge his way past Stone and Batten to score a try, which Paddon failed to convert. Once again Hull rallied and ten minutes before half-time Billy Stone sped down the touch-line and, as reported by the *Yorkshire Post*, 'just as he was tackled, he threw inside to Batten, who tore away at full speed, took a flying leap over Prescott, fell a foot short of the line, and before the defence rallied crept to the line to score.' Kennedy's conversion kick was wide and at half-time the Hornets were leading 7-6. Play in the second half was just as keen as that of the first. Neither side slackened and the tackling was deadly by both sides. Then the Hornets struck again when, from a scrum, Heaton passed to Kynan who quickly transferred to Wild, who served Fitton with a perfect pass. Fitton fooled the approaching Kennedy with a deadly side-step before diving over in the corner to give Rochdale a four-point lead. Incredibly, Hull had the physical and mental reserves to continue, and with ten minutes to play, following a dribble by Taylor and Garrett, Casewell picked up and flung the ball to Dick Taylor for a try in the corner. Hull were a point behind and in the final ten minutes the huge crowd's excitement created a wonderful nerve-wracking atmosphere as the players battled for every yard of the Headingley pitch. Rochdale clung to their slender lead and at full-time were worthy 10-9 winners. At the end of the game all the 26 players realised they had been involved in a classic encounter and in a superb display of sincere sportsmanship spent many minutes congratulating and commiserating each other. It was reported that on the trains taking the supporters home the talk was of what a superb game of football they had witnessed.

Jack Bennett, the Rochdale Hornets captain. The Hornets players received a magnificent reception when their train steamed into Rochdale station, and when Bennett emerged with the cup he was greeted with a great roar of welcome from the huge crowds outside the station. The players and officials boarded two charabancs which drove them through the town's crowded streets to the Town Hall where they enjoyed a reception with the mayor, Alderman Diggle.

Chapter 6

THE 1920S AND THE 1922 TITLE CHANGE TO RUGBY LEAGUE

Billy Stone (left) and Jim Humphries on the Boulevard pitch following Humphries's first-team debut for Hull in September 1920. Humphries made 28 appearances and scored eight tries for the Airlie Birds.

A caricature of Hull winger William 'Billy' Stone. Billy worked as a blacksmith in the Forest of Dean village of Bream and signed for Hull in late 1919 when their scouts saw him playing for the local Rugby Union club. Billy was an immensely fast and talented centre or winger and made 222 appearances, scoring 149 tries for Hull, he gained eight caps for Great Britain and six for England and toured Australia and New Zealand in 1920.

The referee leads the Dewsbury team onto the field at Crown Flatt for the Yorkshire Cup second-round tie again Halifax. Billy Rhodes, the Dewsbury captain, carries the ball. A huge crowd of 26,000 packed into the little ground perched high above the town and witnessed a 'superb thrilling cup tie'. Dewsbury took the lead with an audacious move

by Joe Lyman described by the *Leeds Mercury* thus: 'A penalty had been awarded, but instead of placing the ball for the usual kick at goal, Lyman took advantage of the Halifax defenders' lack of vigilance, he tapped the ball with his toe, regathered, and was over the line like a flash before

the opposition realised what was taking place.' Eventually the demoralised Halifax players recovered, and Garforth kicked a fine penalty to make the score 3-2. Dewsbury held their one-point lead with great defensive play and went on to win the game.

A rare selection postcard sent to a Bramley player in 1920. The team travelled together using the extensive rail network at the time.

A collage of photographs from the 1920 Lions tour to Australia and New Zealand, the last to use the name Northern Union. Newspaper reports from the tour suggest the Australian Rugby League officials thought the Northern Union title to be too parochial and recommended the name be changed to the Rugby League.

The programme for the Batley v Hunslet match on Christmas Day 1920.

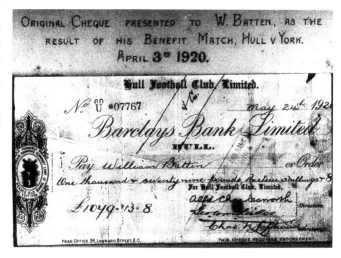

A copy of the cheque that Billy Batten received for his benefit in 1920. The sum of £1,079 13s 8d was a huge amount and demonstrated the high regard the Hull supporters had for Billy.

Broughton Rangers players and officials with the Lancashire Cup in 1920. Back row (left to right): Fernehough, A. Pendleton, H. Templeton, Fred Kennedy, Harry Rebut, E. Fox, H. Taylor, W. Booth. Third row: Fraser, Quigley, Cheetham, Larkin, Richardson, Tomkins, Gatenby. Seated:

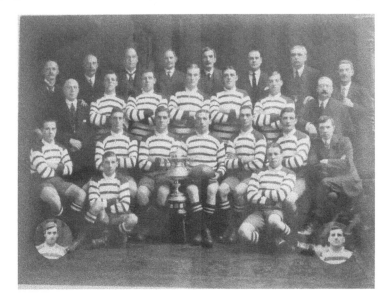

Critchley, Bentham, Davidson, Danson, Barnes, Povey, Miller. Front row: Moss and Hurst. Inserts Scott and Price. The final against Leigh was held at the Willows, Salford, where a crowd of 25,000, including 10,000 from Leigh, gathered. A strong display by the Rangers forwards was described by the *Lancashire Evening Post*: 'The Broughton forwards held a marked superiority and at one period of the game they gained possession almost at will.' Barnes and Price scored tries for Broughton and Higham crossed for Leigh to give the Rangers a 6-3 victory.

Hull with the Championship Trophy in 1920. Back row (left to right): Beasty, Devereaux, Herridge, Caswell, Newsome, Oldham, Humphries. Third row: Wyburn, Garrett, Taylor, Shield, Grice, Holder, Melville. Seated: Boynton, Holdsworth, Batten, Kennedy, Milner, Markham, Lofthouse. Front row: Francis and Hulme.

Hull opposed Huddersfield in the Championship final at Headingley, where a poor crowd of 12,900 gathered on a dull and cloudy Leeds afternoon. Huddersfield had previously won three cups during the season and a victory would have given them a record All Four Cups for the second time. However, the Fartowners were without Wagstaff, Clark, Gronow, Rogers and Thomas, who were all involved in the 1920 Lions tour to Australia and New Zealand. Hull were missing Billy Stone, also on tour, and Devereaux and Caswell through injury and Beasty, Herridge and Newsome, who were suspended. They also lost the services of Alf Grice when he was sent off for tripping shortly before half-time, an action he denied after the match claiming it was mistaken identity. With so many key players missing, the match was hardly a classic, and on a heavy Headingley pitch soon developed in a defensive struggle between the forwards. Huddersfield took the lead in the 27th minute when Major Holland kicked a penalty goal after Billy Batten was caught offside at a scrum. Batten argued with referee Hestford that his position yards away but level with the scrum was onside. The decision stood. The teams changed sides at half-time, with Huddersfield holding a slender 2-0 lead.

With eight minutes of play remaining, a few seconds of brilliance from Billy Batten won the game for Hull when young reserve-team player Markham was about to be tackled, and as described by the *Hull Daily Mail*, 'Markham was already tacked when he both saw and heard Batten tearing along and yelling for the ball. Somehow the junior kept his head and managed to lob out a difficult pass to his centre, it was a most thrilling movement as Batten gathered a difficult ball and tried to annihilate the 20 yards to the line, the Hull centre was practically caught up to ten feet of the line, when he forestalled the impending tackle by that last great leap in which he beat the defence, and grounded the ball over the line with arms and body stretched to their full limit.'

A Wigan team pictured at Leigh on Christmas Day 1920. The full line-up is not known but some players have been identified. Back row: extreme left Percy Coldrick, next to him Fred Roffey, third player from right Bert Webster, extreme right Dick Ramsdale. Front row: captain Sid Jerram and to his left Tommy Howley.

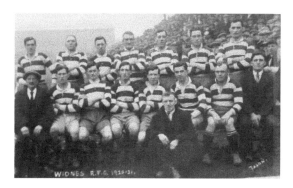

A Widnes team from 1920/21. Back row (left to right): J O'Garra, W Reid, Beswick, H. O'Garra, T. H. Higgins, Blackmore, A. Johnson. Seated: G. Wright (trainer), H. Young, F. Stockley, Brassington, J. Kelly, C. Redman, Townsend, A. Cain. Front row: J. 'Nugget' Noon.

Widnes, Lancashire League winners in 1920.

Widnes were the Lancashire League champions, winning 15 of their 22 fixtures to end the season with 31 points, a single point above nearest rivals Rochdale Hornets and Oldham. Widnes had a superb defence throughout the season, only conceding 83 points, the best performance in the competition.

Arthur Moore and Billy Stone spin a coin before the Hull derby game at Craven Street in 1920/21.

A Wigan Highfield team from the 1920/21 season.

The Batley team, reserves and officials pictured before the league game at Wakefield Trinity on 12 February 1921. This also served as the joint benefit game for Wakefield players Herbert Kershaw and George Taylor. Standing (left to right): Mr Frederic Wilfrid Hoyle Auty (vice-president), Mr Lewis, S. Boocock (treasurer), Mr Jack Sutcliffe (trainer-coach), Tom Harkness, J. Ashton, Tom Wynward, Willie Gray, B. Hartley, Fred Willis, W. H. 'Bill' Goosey, Joe Robinson, Dr William Walker (vice-president), George Ramsbottom and Mr Kershaw Newsome (committee). Sitting: Alan Mortimer, Harry Rees, David Evans (captain), Will Price, T. Davis and Percy Hargreaves. Front row: Ivor Jones, Bryn Williams and Ike Fowler.

A caricature of Hull FC forward Bob Taylor. Hull signed Taylor from Barrow in January 1920. The highly mobile second row forward soon became a firm favourite of the Boulevard crowds. 'Dear Old Bob' made 308 appearances for Hull and scored 164 tries during his ten-year career with the Airlie Birds.

A Rochdale Hornets team from 1921. The names of the players are not known.

Hull Kingston Rovers and the Australian tourists in action at Craven Street on 24 September 1921.

Fine weather and sunshine in East Hull attracted a good crowd of 13,000 for the tour game. The Rovers played well in the first quarter of the game, their forwards rushing tactics and keen tackling breaking up the tourists' passing movements. Eventually, the Kangaroos took control and Blinkhorn, Grey and Horder crossed for tries and Norman kicked two goals. Bradshaw kicked a goal for the Rovers and at half-time the tourists were leading 13-2. Bradshaw added two goals early in the second half. Later Harold Horder produced a bewildering display of high-speed handling and running expertise to score three tries. The *Hull Daily Mail* described his play as follows: 'In swerving and side stepping he loses no

pace but appears to do it all in one movement. The again, if there was a difficult ball to gather either in the air or from the ground, he managed to somehow obtain possession even whilst travelling at a terrific rate.' The Hull football enthusiasts gave Horder a magnificent ovation of cheering and applause to his display. The game ended 26-6 to the tourists with one blemish when the visitors' Shultz was sent-off for striking a Rovers player.

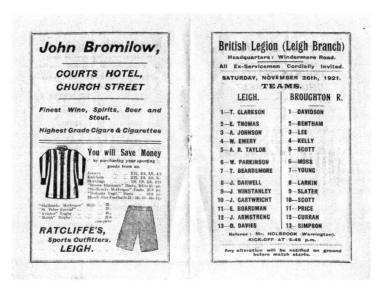

Pages from the Leigh v Broughton Rangers programme, 1921. Programmes had become a regular feature at games in the 1920s and advertising revenue helped to supplement a club's income.

H Edwards, G Norrey, T Worsley, J Tonge.
T Wild, J Key, S Jones, T Crossley, R Crowshaw.
J Scholes, J Bailey, H Worsley, H Unsworth, S Howarth, J Smith, B Britton, D Jones, B Kearns.
D Cullis, J Arnold, T Smith, J Dawson, B Price, H Powell, F Evans, B Rees.
J Evans, H Halsall, A Jenkins.

Swinton in 1920/21.

A photograph of the Australian tourists presented to Swinton to commemorate the tour game on 16 November 1921.

The team members published in the official programme for the Swinton v Australia tour match.

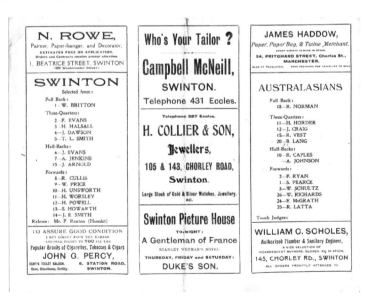

SWINTON V AUSTRALIANS NOV. 16TH 1921

SWINTON — 9. Prs.
Australians —— NIL.

We have'nt got a war cry, we have'nt got a dance
But that dos'nt say we are not a race of fighters
And we're glad the days arrived, when we have a bloomin chance
To have a go at these old Aussie Blighters
We are dangerous at hay, we are merciful as well
And for them, its perhaps a good job too
And just to finish up with, did anyone ever hear tell
Of a Lion that had funked a KANGAROO.

One of the best performances of last season, was ours when we
beat the Australian Team. One of our players Harry Whitehead, in
honor of this event, drew a very clever cartoon. a reduced copy of
which we here reproduce.

An illustration celebrating Swinton's victory over the 1921 Kangaroos.

Heavy rain fell throughout the game at the Chorley Road ground, which reduced the attendance to 6,000. The town was also in the financial grip of a long-running coal dispute which also affected the attendance. The Lions were at full strength but the Kangaroos had made several changes and were missing some key players. Swinton began the game at a ferocious pace, tearing into the tourists, the *Hull Daily Mail* commenting, 'Playing a robust, determined game, the Swinton forwards rarely gave the Australians a chance to attain a balance, controlling the ball very effectively, with their backs spotting and tackling fearlessly in support.' The Lions opened the scoring with a fine penalty goal from Billy Britton. Swinton soon launched an attack described by the *Manchester Evening News* thus: 'Swinton kept up the pressure and because of magnificent work the home side scored the finest try recorded against the Australians so far. A passing movement was started by Howarth, and others who took part were Worsley, J. Evans and Frank Evans. The last named tricked several opponents and ran over for an unconverted try.' At half-time Swinton were leading by five points. The tourists were struggling with the constant rain, slippery ball and heavy pitch and their expected fight-back never really materialised. The brilliant South Sydney wing man, Harold Horder, did his utmost to inspire his teammates, but the Lions were aware of his abilities and their keen spotting and tackling kept him well under control. Billy Britton added two more penalty goals in the second half and the Lions of Swinton were well-deserved 9-0 victors and the only club side to prevent the Kangaroos scoring during the 36-match tour.

A Batley team in 1921/22 during their last season under the title Northern Rugby Football Union. Players in kit (left to right): Hugh 'Bob' Murray, Harry Rees, David Evans, Ike Fowler, unknown, Willie Brennan, George Kilby, Will Price, George Ramsbottom, Willie Scott, Allen Mortimer, George Douglas and Fred Carter.

Batley finished the season in sixth place in the Championship with 48 points and in second place in the Yorkshire League. Forward George Ramsbottom gained two Yorkshire caps during the season when he opposed Lancashire at Rochdale and Cumberland at Halifax.

Dinny Campbell waves goodbye as he leaves Leeds Railway Station on 22 April 1921. The Australian centre was a popular member of the Leeds team during the nine seasons he spent at Headingley. On his arrival in Australia, Campbell played one last season for Eastern Suburbs and on his

retirement he maintained his links with Leeds and was involved in several top-class Australian players joining them.

The front cover of a Northern Union Annual for the 1921/22 final season.

BIBLIOGRAPHY

The following books have been consulted during the compilation of this book:

The Roots of Rugby League, Trevor Delaney

The Grounds of Rugby League, Trevor Delaney

Rugby's Great Split, Tony Collins

1895 and All That, Tony Collins

The Lions of Swinton, Stephen Wild

Swinton Lions 150 Years, Stephen Wild

Images of Sport: Swinton Lions, Stephen Wild

Halifax Rugby League the First Hundred Years, Andrew Hardcastle

Images of Huddersfield Rugby League Club, David Gronow

Huddersfield RLFC 100 Greats, David Gronow

Rugby League in Manchester, Graham Morris

The King of Brilliance (James Lomas), Graham Morris

The Rugby League Myth, Michael Latham and Tom Mather

Buff Berry and the Mighty Bongers, Michael Latham

Old Faithful, Michael Ulyatt and Bill Dalton

All Blacks to All Golds, John Haynes.

Best in the Northern Union, Tom Mather

Tries in the Valleys, Peter Lush and Dave Farrar

The Robins, Graham Pugh

Trinity, Mike Rylance

The Kangaroos, Ian Heads

Making Up the Numbers, Stuart Sheard

The Rugby League Records Keepers Club History of Rugby League Booklets 1895 to 1922, Irvine Saxton

Newspapers:

Athletic News

Yorkshire Post

Hull Daily Mail

Midlands Daily Telegraph

Manchester Guardian

Manchester Evening News

Leeds Mercury

Northern Whig

Yorkshire Evening News

Yorkshire Press

ND - #0276 - 270225 - C0 - 234/156/14 - PB - 9781780915852 - Gloss Lamination